Everything
I Know About God

I've Learned From Being
A Parent

Published by
The Bible Reading Fellowship
15 The Chambers, Vineyard
Abingdon, OX14 3FE
United Kingdom
Tel: +44 (0)1865 319700
Email: enquiries@brf.org.uk
Website: www.brf.org.uk
BRF is a Registered Charity

ISBN 978 1 84101 416 6

First published 2013

10 9 8 7 6 5 4 3 2 1 0

Acknowledgments
Unless otherwise stated, scripture quotations are taken from The New Revised Standard
Version of the Bible, Anglicized Edition, copyright © 1989, 1995 by the Division of Christian
Education of the National Council of the Churches of Christ in the USA, and are used by
permission. All rights reserved.

Scripture quotations taken from the New Jerusalem Bible, published and copyright © 1985
by Darton, Longman and Todd Ltd and les Editions du Cerf, and by Doubleday, a division of
Bantam Doubleday Dell Publishing Group, Inc. Used by permission of Darton, Longman and
Todd Ltd, and Doubleday, a division of Random House, Inc.

A catalogue record for this book is available from the British Library

The paper used in the production of this publication was supplied by mills that source their
raw materials from sustainable managed forests. Soy-based inks were used in its printing and
the laminate film is biodegradable.

Printed in Singapore by Craft Print International Ltd

Everything
I Know About God

I've Learned From Being
A Parent

Veronica Zundel

To my mother
Jenny Zundel
1915–2012

Acknowledgments

*This book is all my own work and I'm not going to blame anyone
else for what's in it, but I'd still like to give my thanks
to John for letting himself be named,
to the late Margaret Granowski and to the very much alive
Roz Hewitt for gently steering me towards better mental health,
to Ed for nearly 24 years of supporting me in that journey,
to my church for 20 years of reminding me
that 'God is nice and he likes us',
and to Naomi Starkey and her team for quite a few years
of thoughtful and considerate editiing.
And, of course, to both my late parents for all their love,
and to God for being nice and liking me.*

Contents

Introduction

This book is the story of my journey into and through parenthood. This journey was not an easy one, and it continues to be full of difficulties. Not only did I suffer from infertility and finally have a child at the age of 41 (making me an 'elderly primigravida'!) but the course of my son's development has not been the same as that of most children. This has meant that my husband and I as his parents have had to fight many battles on his behalf, and continue to do so.

One thing I rapidly discovered was that you don't learn to be a parent all at once and then exercise what you've learned. Your child changes and learns every day, and every day you have to reassess how you are relating to it. Parenting courses are all very well, and we did several, which helped us cope. However, as a parent you are basically always making it up as you go along, because your child, whether or not it has a 'special need', is unique. My mother at 96 is still discovering things about me she didn't know before! Being a parent is a constant progress of rethinking and adapting, and while the pace of change may slow down, it never stops.

As I grew into parenthood, I began to see parallels between how I behaved and felt towards my beloved child, and how God might feel and behave towards me and God's other children. I spotted more and more connections between my attitude towards my son John and what might be God's attitude to us, God's children. I also started to look afresh at things I had been taught in my Christian life, and to ask,

'Would a good parent really do this?' It was not far from this to the conclusion: if God is at least as loving a parent as we should be to our children, then we have to rethink some of the things we believe about God, because the actions we sometimes attribute to God are actions no loving parent would perform.

My original plan was to structure the book around theological themes such as creation, fall, redemption and recreation. Instead, I have chosen to build it around stages of child development, from conception to adulthood. This is because my thinking about God's parenthood has arisen out of my own experience, not out of a doctrinal blueprint, and I found I wanted the book to do the same. I think you'll find I end up saying quite a lot about creation, fall and the rest in any case!

Regardless of whether or not you are a parent, or would like to be, or even wish you hadn't been, I hope this book can help you think about God's parenthood. The writer of the epistle to the Ephesians calls God 'the Father, from whom every family in heaven and on earth takes its name' (Ephesians 3:14–15). If earthly families gain their nature from God's fatherhood, might it not work the other way round too—might our experience of family, especially of bringing up our own family, not tell us something about the nature of God? That is the question on which this book is founded. And I hope it supplies a few tentative answers.

A note about language

I belong to a church that produced an 'inclusive language' policy in 1986—around the time Christians were just beginning to discover how exclusive their language had felt for

7

many women. Many of us no longer use 'he', 'his' and 'him' to refer to all of humanity (or indeed refer to all of humanity as 'man' or 'mankind'). The main reason is that this language implies that the default state of humanity is male, and that women are a subgroup, when in fact women are a slight majority in the world. Some of us also feel that we no longer wish to refer to God exclusively in male pronouns, because God is beyond male and female, and both sexes are fully in God's image.

For this reason I have chosen to refer to children mainly as 'it' in this book, and sometimes I have alternated between male and female pronouns for children or parents. As for God, rather than using 's/he', which sounds a little as if I were uncertain about God's gender, I have chosen mostly to repeat the name 'God' rather than using a pronoun. I hope this isn't irritating to the reader.

The Finnish language makes no distinction in its pronouns between male and female. This is why, if you know someone Finnish, you may find they sometimes refer to a woman as 'he' or a man as 'she'—they get confused because their language doesn't have this distinction in pronouns. It may also be why Finnish women appear to be so strong and self-confident! Their language has never told them they were 'the second sex'.

In English we don't have a gender neutral pronoun other than 'it'—and I certainly don't want to refer to God as 'it'. So I have done my best and tried to use whatever language sounded most natural. Please forgive me where I've failed.

Chapter 1

Conception

Tests

It was a blazing August day, and for some reason I had woken up with an unexplained fever. I felt awful, but I knew I had to drag myself to the local hospital for an NHS fertility appointment. I had been waiting 18 months for it and I wasn't prepared to miss it now.

I staggered to the bus and managed to get myself up to the right department. The first thing that happened was that the receptionist shoved a printed sheet into my hand, explaining that the fertility clinic had been reduced from two days a week to one, in order to put more resources into the abortion clinic. I was livid, as well as feverish. Didn't they know how painful it was for a woman desperate to have a baby to be confronted with the situation of those who don't want theirs? And fertility tests have to be done at certain times in a woman's monthly cycle—how were they going to coordinate that with a one-day-a-week clinic? It could be a year before my dates and theirs lined up.

I felt like shouting, 'Why don't you just cut out the middle woman, cancel both clinics and let the infertile women have the babies the unwillingly pregnant are currently aborting?' There I sat, fuming, still with a temperature, in the badly ventilated waiting room. After about 45 minutes I was called through, but, rather than being seen at once, I was put in a cubicle where I waited another half hour or so, while nurses and administrators rushed to and fro saying things like, 'Where have you put the new one?' and 'Have you got papers for the new one?' I knew that meant me, but I felt I was being treated as less than a person—what a contrast to the private clinics where we had already had tests (thanks to my generous parents), and where we were given real coffee and I was called 'Ms Zundel'.

Finally, I saw the doctor and was not much reassured. She wanted to repeat all the tests we had already paid for, which would take months, and to give me a laparoscopy, which the private doctor had already shown to be unnecessary. I was nearly 40 and didn't have that sort of time. At this point I gave up and said, 'Forget it. We'll continue with the private treatment.'

Now, I'm not knocking the National Health Service. My father served in it as a specialist physician for nearly 40 years, and I am a staunch, if not always consistent, supporter of state healthcare. I tell you all this not to demonstrate how inadequate the NHS is—when I later had breast cancer it was superb—but to share some of the constant, nagging pain of infertility.

Before I got married, and for a while after, I thought I was pretty neutral about having children. I liked my career and I was a bit scared about how I would cope with being a parent. It sounded like such a lot of work! But when my husband Ed and I started 'trying', and nothing happened, the impact it had on my emotions was intense. I had waited long years to get married, finally marrying on my 36th birthday, and now it seemed there was yet one more aspect of 'normal' life that I wasn't going to be granted. I had never, in my single years, been particularly desperate to have children, although anxious to have a partner, but now the biological clock was approaching midnight and I longed to be 'in the flow of life'.

We had been getting increasingly unhappy with the Anglican church to which we belonged and had been trying other churches. As soon as we arrived at the Mennonite church (then the only Mennonite congregation in the UK, and reasonably near our home), I had an emotional 'crash', for which our struggles with fertility were a triggering factor. I think I must have felt I was now in a safe place to have the breakdown I had been expecting for years. I had suffered periodic depression since my university days, but this was a great deal worse, with constant impulses to harm myself drastically.

Wood Green Mennonite Church also proved to be a place where we could talk freely about our fertility issues; in our previous church we knew there were other couples living with the same issues, but somehow it was never mentioned. Why is infertility such a taboo topic? Is it because it undermines the convenient theology that God will give us everything we ask for?

Weird stuff

I gradually recovered, with the help of the right medication. After a false start I also found a lovely Christian therapist who would be my lifeline for the next ten years. And we carried on 'trying'—it can be rather fun sometimes (although not when you have to wake up early mumbling, 'We have to do it right now, we've got a post-coital test in an hour'!)

This is where the weird stuff comes in. During this time a counsellor gave me the book *Healing the Family Tree* by Dr Kenneth McAll.[1] It's a strange book, which relates how the late Dr McAll used to look at people's family trees and identify 'problem' deaths in them which had not been properly mourned, such as a miscarriage, or a suicide who was buried in unconsecrated ground, or deaths in war when there was no funeral. He would then lead a simple requiem communion service for the people identified, together with the person/people who had come to him for help. As a result there would often be dramatic healing, including of psychiatric illnesses, in his clients.

Now I have an 'interesting' family tree, being the daughter of Viennese Holocaust survivors. My husband Ed and I both read the book, and we agreed that if even half of the miracles recounted in the book were true, it was worth thinking about. More than that, we both came to the conclusion independently that we should hold a memorial service for my maternal grandmother, who perished in a concentration camp in 1942, long before I was born. Although infertility obviously can't be inherited, my grandmother had in fact been infertile and had adopted my mother. So there was a sense in which my inability to conceive felt as if it was 'inherited' from her.

Ed and I spent around a year preparing for this service by investigating both of our family trees, helped by work that had been done by our respective aunts. In the course of interrogating my mother for this purpose, I discovered many family secrets. There was the adoptive cousin who was a professional clairvoyant and who was called to tell Hitler's fortune and, when Hitler didn't like it, was shot dead by the SS. (There are three films and at least one book about this cousin.) There was the adoptive great-great-aunt who, in 1938, when the Nazis moved into Vienna, killed herself at the age of 88. Perhaps most intriguing of all, there was my mother's adoptive grandmother, of whom she had never spoken before, but who, by my mother's account, made her daughters' lives a misery. Strangely, she had two daughters—my grandmother and great-aunt—neither of whom could have children. (Of course medical science was not advanced enough then to tell whether it was these women or their husbands who were infertile.)

The biggest feature I noticed about my family tree, on both my mother's and my father's sides, was that at my generation, it just stopped. My mother was an only adopted child and her aunt had no children. My father's sister was single all her life, and his brother, despite two marriages and a long-term mistress, never had any legitimate children (although there's a 'wrong side of the blanket' daughter a little older than me, whose existence I only discovered when I was in my 30s and whose full name I still don't know). So I have never had any first cousins, while my brother died unmarried and childless, and here was I unable to conceive. The only branch of the family that was actually continuing was that of my Hungarian second cousins, who had several children and who are incidentally (or perhaps not so incidentally?) Christians. In every other direction my family tree seemed to be dying out. No wonder I was eager to continue the family line!

We planned to hold the service for my grandmother on the date of my late brother's birthday in late November—it just seemed right. (My brother committed suicide in 1975 and I have always thought of him as a second-generation Holocaust victim.) Because of the availability of the Anglican vicar whom we wanted to conduct the service, we had to make it a day later. Imagine my amazement when it turned out that my then regular retreat centre was having a weekend on 'Healing the family tree' two days before the day we'd fixed! I had to go to this, of course.

In the first session I found myself sitting next to a woman who not only turned out to live near me and employ the same cleaner, but had also lived through a brother's suicide. Halfway through the weekend, when both she and I had some quibbles about what the speaker was saying and doing (I'm not sure I believe in 'pre-conception consciousness'!), we agreed to leave a session and go off to pray on our own. She then told me she had something of a ministry of praying for people who wanted to have babies. 'Curioser and curioser,' as Alice in Wonderland said...[2]

I came back home, and two days later we had the service for my grandmother and her sister, in the chapel of the London Mennonite Centre, with a photograph of my grandmother on display and both my parents present. It was a quiet, low-key affair, and immediately afterwards I thought no more about it—in fact, I had stopped thinking about the possible connection between my grandmother's infertility and mine, and felt the service was worth doing just to lay my grandmother to rest. At this stage we had already been told what kind of treatment we were advised, and the hormones were being kept cool in the fridge until it was time to take them.

But... only a couple of weeks later I began to feel a bit odd, as though I had some sort of stomach upset. It was a particular kind of feeling that I had had only once before, when my period had been late and I had thought that I might be pregnant, only to be disappointed days later.

Yet I still didn't 'join the dots' and work out what might be happening. It was only when I rang up a local clinic to arrange an X-ray of my coccyx, which I had damaged in an ice-skating accident, and the receptionist asked when my last period had been, that I did a quick calculation and realised, to my own surprise, that it was five weeks ago. This would not have been unusual in earlier years, but I had become quite regular in my middle age. Could this be 'it'? Nervously, I purchased a pregnancy test and, even more nervously, tried it out over the weekend. This is a bad idea, by the way, because then you have to wait until at least Monday to see your doctor.

Would you believe it? The little line was pink (or maybe blue, I forget these things). I couldn't really take it in it till I'd seen the GP, but the evidence was unmistakably there. I was pregnant. In fact, we worked out later that the baby must have been conceived on the afternoon I came home from the 'Healing the family tree' weekend, between that and the service on the Tuesday. Not every mother can be that accurate! I immediately stopped the anti-depressants I was taking. (Please don't try this at home, as psychiatric medication should always be reduced gradually, but I was on such a low dose that my psychiatrist called it a 'homeopathic dose'.)

I never had that coccyx X-ray. My lovely dad said, 'The X-ray wouldn't have made it better anyway.' My news came just before Christmas, and we told my parents on Christmas Eve, the day we Austrians give our presents. We went out for Christmas Day dinner that year, and the food was actually awful, but no one cared because we were all so happy. It was certainly early days, but I had the conviction that this baby was staying. By the way, the hormones are still somewhere in my garden shed—I think they must have expired by now.

The God who yearns

Why have I told you this long and detailed story? What does it have to do with thinking about God's parenthood of us? Here's what I think.

Many medieval and earlier theologians spoke of God as 'impassible', meaning that God is free of any emotion and unaffected by events. I can see why they came to this conclusion, because in their eyes emotions were a sign of weakness (they were nearly all men, after all!) and God was supposed to be perfect and have no needs.

However, that's not the God I see in the Bible at all. From the beginning of Genesis, when God says, 'Let us make humankind in our image' (1:26), God is about relationship, and relationship means emotional attachment. Even in the story of creation in Genesis, God is repeatedly 'pleased' with what has been made; and what is pleasure but an emotion?

Traditionally, the idea of God's making humanity in God's own image has been interpreted to mean that human beings have 'reason'—the power of consciousness and reflection— just as God does. This, theologians have said, is what distinguishes us from animals. Unfortunately, it has also been used to establish the idea that men are made more in the image of God than women, since men were once thought to have more 'reason'. (The fact that women weren't as well educated as men seems to have been ignored.) Male theologians, believing that their 'logical and rational' thought was a reflection of God, denigrated women as too full of wayward emotions to reflect God fully. Quite a few church leaders still seem to think this way today, judging from some of the kind of contributions that have been made to the debate about women's ordination.

What if the 'image of God' was located not in our reasoning power, but in our capacity for love and relationship? What if my passionate yearning for a child was a mirror to God's passionate yearning for relationship with me and all God's other children?

We talk of God as a Trinity of persons in relationship. The Trinity is of course a mystery, of which the reality is far beyond our imaginations. What does it mean to be three in one, and one in three? Our minds cannot grasp it, but at the very least it tells us that it's in the very nature of God to be in relationship, and that relationship is a relationship of love, mutual outpouring and the flow of life. Is it too far-fetched to say that the very nature of God makes it inevitable that God must create life which can reflect God and love God in return?

I am not saying here that God *had* to create the universe. That would be to say that God was in some way inadequate without creation. (As the apostle Paul might say, I speak as a child here, from my inevitably limited understanding of what it could mean to be the all-sufficient God.) Neither am I drawing the parallel that my life was inadequate without a child, although that was the way it had felt. Many people choose to be childless, or live a life that is fruitful in many other ways, even though they could not bear a child. Many adopt or foster the unwanted or uncared-for children of others, and give them a chance in life they would never have had otherwise—and I have seen at first hand how costly that choice can be, and the potential trauma of bringing up a child who has been permanently damaged by an abusive environment in their early years.

What I *am* saying is that, since we are told by the first epistle of John that 'God is love' (1 John 4:8), it was inevitable that God would want to express that love in making free, independent creatures who could love God back. There is no such thing as love that does not relate to another. Even when we say we love ourselves (and there is nothing wrong in caring for yourself), we are in a sense treating ourselves as if we were the neighbour we are called to love. The letter to the Ephesians says, 'No one ever hates his own body, but he nourishes and tenderly cares for it' (5:29).

There is no criticism implied here. God wants us to look after the bodies God has given us. That is one of the reasons why the current epidemic of self-harming behaviour among young people is so tragic. Instead, our love for our own bodies is meant to spill over to love of our neighbour: 'You shall love your neighbour as yourself' (Matthew 22:39).

Love by its very nature is relationship, and if God is love, God is relationship too. I believe that God not only identified utterly with my feelings of devastation at my infertility, but did so out of God's own experience of longing for children, and God's pain when those children are (as most of humanity is) alienated from God—which, I have to say, is mind-boggling.

The hurting God

Does this make God too 'human'? (I've never understood why being human was supposed to be a failing.) Are we wrong to attribute emotions and desires to God? The Bible would suggest otherwise. What we find in the Old Testament is a God full of emotions towards God's chosen people: a God who gets angry, who 'repents' of destructive plans, who longs for righteousness in the world and among God's people. Consider this passage from Isaiah 42:

The Lord goes forth like a soldier,
like a warrior he stirs up his fury;
he cries out, he shouts aloud,
he shows himself mighty against his foes.

For a long time I have held my peace,
I have kept still and restrained myself;
now I will cry out like a woman in labour,
I will gasp and pant. (vv. 13–14)

Here, God is a campaigner for righteousness, angry at the injustice of the world, and a woman in labour, desperate for her child to be born and her pains to be over. The 'child' is the new, redeemed world that God wants to establish, a world of which the Israelites are meant to be a forerunner, and God cannot wait for it to emerge. The idea of God gasping and panting in labour is a far cry from the 'strong and silent' God of many of the traditional theologians.

Or take an almost throwaway verse in Deuteronomy, a book not noted for displays of emotion:

Although heaven and the heaven of heavens belong to the Lord your God, the earth with all that is in it, yet the Lord set his heart in love on your ancestors alone and chose you, their descendants after them, out of all the peoples, as it is today. (10:14–15)

'The Lord set his heart in love'—does that sound like a God who has no emotions, no desire for God's creation or any of its human inhabitants? If God is unaffected by emotion, how can God have even a metaphorical 'heart'? Have you ever heard of a person who loved others but didn't feel affected in any way by what the others said and did?

Some parts of the Bible even portray God as being moved, by external circumstances or people, to change plans. In Genesis, for instance, God 'repents' of having made human beings when God looks at how corrupt they have become:

The Lord saw that the wickedness of humankind was great in the earth, and that every inclination of the thoughts of their hearts was only evil continually. And the Lord was sorry that he had made humankind on the earth, and it grieved him to his heart. So the Lord said, 'I will blot out from the earth the human beings I have created—people together with animals and creeping things and birds of the air, for I am sorry that I have made them.' (6:5–7)

Here we have a God who feels anger and pain at a broken universe; a God who is delighted to find one person who lives the right way: 'But Noah found favour in the sight of the Lord' (v. 8).

Exodus 32 shows Moses pleading with God to take back God's anger at the faithlessness of the Israelites:

But Moses implored the Lord his God, and said, 'O Lord, why does your wrath burn hot against your people, whom you brought out of the land of Egypt with great power and with a mighty hand? Why should the Egyptians say, "It was with evil intent that he brought them out to kill them in the mountains, and to consume them from the face of the earth"? Turn from your fierce wrath; change your mind and do not bring disaster on your people.' ... And the Lord changed his mind about the disaster that he planned to bring on his people. (vv. 11–12, 14)

Jesus wept

In the Gospels too, Jesus, who is 'the image of the invisible God' (Colossians 1:15), is moved with deep emotion when he contemplates the grave of his dead friend Lazarus: 'When Jesus saw [Mary] weeping, and the Jews who came with her also weeping, he was greatly disturbed in spirit and deeply moved'. (John 11:33). The Greek, I gather, means literally something like 'his gut was wrenched'.

Jesus loved Lazarus and his sisters Mary and Martha (v. 5). He also had an inner circle of disciples, Peter, James and John. He even had one disciple who is repeatedly described as 'the disciple whom Jesus loved': 'One of his disciples— the one whom Jesus loved—was reclining next to him' (John 13:23). Confronted by a rich young man, Jesus' response is as follows: 'Jesus, looking at him, loved him' (Mark 10:21).

Jesus, the image of God, experienced human emotions all the way from anger to delight, and none of these made him a sinner.

Does God have favourites? The Bible seems to suggest it and, being born Jewish, I might like to think this is the case. Of course, God's love for all his creatures is infinite and can't be more for one creature than another. Yet there is still a sense in which particular acts of God appear to show a particular love for the recipients of those acts. This again is in the nature of love. I am called to love everyone in general, as God loves, but I still have a particular love for my child above all others. I would be very taken aback if my husband told me he loved me in general, just as he loves the rest of humanity, with no particular preference for me as myself. Human love is inevitably particular, and that is no shame to humans. I have only one child, but if I had more than one, I hope I would love each of them equally, and yet I would still love each of them in a different way, because they would be different people.

William Paul Young expresses this beautifully in his million-selling book *The Shack*.[3] The character (who is female and black!) standing for God the father has a habit of saying,

'I am especially fond of [insert name of character]'. When asked if there is anyone in the world she is not especially fond of, she is unable to think of anyone.

Humans can love only one or two people—well, maybe a dozen or two, if you have a big family—at that intimate level, because our love is so limited. It is not so with God, whose love is infinite. I suspect that God loves everyone in particular: God's infinite love for you is different from God's infinite love for the person next door—not because God has different feelings towards you and them, but because you are different from them. God's general love for all humankind is specific to every human being. Love is particular, but infinite love is particular to everyone.

The childless God

Could it be that the longing I felt to have a child, to be in the flow of handing on life, is just a pale copy of the longing God has felt, from infinity to infinity, for a creation to love and creatures in it who would mirror God's love? Could it be that God was not lonely or bored or wanted puppets with which to play, but that the Trinity, a God who is defined by relationship, chose to make a world to love out of the overflowing of the love that was within God?

I can't prove it—all our ideas about God are approximate guesses—but I think that God entered with me into my struggle with childlessness, because God experienced something like childlessness too, longing for a world and especially for a creature that, by its nature, would reflect God and be able to come to know God. So 'Father' is not just the name Jesus used for God, but is God's name from eternity; it is inherent in the 'Godness of God' that God would bring forth a world, and that world would be populated with, and 'managed' by, children of God, looking (as all birth children do) like their parent. The difference is that God had the power to make that world simply by speaking: 'Then God said, "Let there be light"; and there was light' (Genesis 1:3). We, however, regardless of how creative we are, don't have the power to make a child just by deciding we want one. Even the latest fertility treatments carry no guarantees.

So that's my first 'deduction about God' from my experiences of infertility and healing. The human desire to pass on life, to create something that has never existed before and relate to it, is not just a case of 'selfish genes' manipulating us to replicate them. It is a mirror image of the desire God has to share God's love with created beings and their world. There are many other ways to express our God-given creativity than having children, but it's one of the best—and the most life-changing and all-absorbing.

Chapter 2

Pregnancy and birth

'Blooming'

We were driving to my parents' house, which is ten minutes' drive from ours. Halfway there we had to stop the car by the verge on a busy two-way road, so that I could throw up on the grass. Isn't pregnancy fun? I was sick not just in the mornings, but all day every day. In fact, the evenings were the worst. Every morning before I could get out of bed, my long-suffering husband had to bring me fresh-cooked semolina, which was the only thing I could face. Apart from this, I lived mainly on Bath Oliver biscuits, which were bland enough not to upset my stomach.

Then, just as if a tap had been turned off, I sat at home one Friday night when I was 14 weeks pregnant and realised that I did not feel sick any more. I think my baby must have read the pregnancy books along with me, as he seemed to do everything exactly at the right time, including stopping making me sick!

The books also told me I would be 'blooming' during the second trimester. Unfortunately, I took this for granted and foolishly tried to write a book while pregnant. I ended up getting depressed again from the stress. I had to go back on anti-depressants, which was a disappointment, and I worried about how they would affect the baby, although I was assured it was safe.

Meanwhile I followed the 'pregnancy diary' books to find

out how big and how developed my baby was at each stage, and was amazed at the first flutter of his movements. (Later, of course, he became expert at kicking me in the bladder…)

I did manage to 'bloom' quite a lot during the last three months. I was as big as the side of a house; it was a hot summer, and being pregnant is like having a little furnace burning inside you. I spent a lot of time lying on a sun lounger in the garden eating ice cream, drinking Ribena (which was another of my cravings) and reading novels. I am also rather proud of the fact that I continued driving right up to my last week, although it was getting harder and harder to reach the wheel over my bump! I even preached at my church when very pregnant, which might have shocked some traditionalist churchmen.

We called our 'bump' Jo-Jo, as the name we had for a girl was Joanna, and for a boy John, which is my husband's middle name. (He has his father's middle name and we wanted to start a tradition.) I have to say, I was totally convinced that the baby was going to turn out to be Joanna!

Being pregnant gave me a whole new dimension to the much-loved Psalm 139:

It was you who formed my inward parts;
you knit me together in my mother's womb.
I praise you, for I am fearfully and wonderfully made.
Wonderful are your works; that I know very well.
My frame was not hidden from you,
when I was being made in secret,
intricately woven in the depths of the earth (vv. 13–15)

Not only was I 'getting to know' the little creature inside me, who was still such a stranger that I didn't even know his or her sex, but God too was watching over my 'miracle baby' at every stage of his or her development. It's such a strange feeling knowing that one is 'making' a new human being, yet without any effort on one's own part. The baby was being formed by my body, yet in another sense God was doing all the making.

Elsewhere the Bible suggests our relationship to God goes back even further than the womb. Here is how God speaks to the prophet Jeremiah about his calling:

Before I formed you in the womb I knew you,
and before you were born I consecrated you;
I appointed you a prophet to the nations. (1:5)

Perhaps the speaker on that 'Healing the family tree' weekend was not so wrong about her 'pre-conception consciousness'. We may not be conscious before conception but God is conscious of us before we are even a small fertilised blob of dividing cells. And this depth of care is not just a special favour to a prophet. Through Isaiah God speaks to the whole Jewish nation which God has called:

But now hear, O Jacob my servant,
Israel whom I have chosen!
Thus says the Lord who made you,
who formed you in the womb and will help you. (44:1–2)

Here we see God 'knowing' a whole people from their mothers' wombs, and choosing them for a special purpose. Later, Christian interpreters would understand this as prophesying the coming of Jesus, who was named by the angel Gabriel even before he was conceived. Just as the nation of

Israel was called to model right human living to the world, so Jesus' life would model what it means to live in God's righteousness and to be a full human being.

No turning back

Although I was already 40 when I was pregnant, I refused to have an amniocentesis test to find out whether my baby had Down's syndrome. The test itself carried a risk of causing miscarriage, and I was so sure God had sent this baby that I would accept it with whatever condition it came. Little did I know how that commitment would be needed later.

Reading baby books and shopping for baby equipment was both exciting and terrifying. I found it hard to imagine how this new little person with all his accessories—cot, car seat, changing mat, huge quantities of clothes and nappies—was going to fit into our small home.

One thing the baby books told me was that a newborn baby could recognise tunes it had heard regularly while in the womb. One mother told of how her newborn became sleepy as soon as it heard the *EastEnders* theme tune, as she had sat down to relax in front of the soap opera every day during her pregnancy. Inspired by this, I made up a little song to sing to 'Jo-Jo' every day in my bath, but sadly when I sang it to him after he was born, he showed no signs of recognition. Perhaps my powers of composition weren't quite in the league of the *Eastenders* composer? (I can't even remember the song myself now, so it can't have been all that good.)

Recently I heard a very moving story from the youth minister Mark Yaconelli. It is about a popular Christian writer called Morton Kelsey. When Morton was born, he was what was then called a 'blue baby' (he had rhesus disease, which means that the mother's blood type is incompatible with the baby's). His mother thought he was so ugly that she rejected him and refused to care for him, so his parents hired a young local girl, who lived with the baby in an annexe to their home. Once he was three or four, he was sent off to a boarding school, where he was very unhappy. Hardly surprisingly, he had a breakdown at 20 and gave up his faith in God.

God, however, did not give up on him, and he came back to faith later and became a writer. When he was in his mid-70s, he received a letter from an elderly lady in a care home, asking whether he had been born in a certain place in the US and had been cared for after birth by a local girl. This girl, now in her 90s, had seen his name in print and contacted him. Of course, he went to see her as soon as he could and found her frail but still totally *compos mentis*. At the end of his visit, he laid his head on her shoulder and she sang a little song she used to sing to him when he was a toddler. Recognising it, he burst into tears, and they both cried over each other.

Is it too fanciful, or does God sing a song of love over each child as it grows in the womb, a song of which, when we are born, we hear faint echoes in the world around us, if we can stop for long enough to listen? Certainly we can say that just as a wanted baby is loved by its parents even before it is born, so God's love hovers over each human creature from before its life has even started. I think it was Mother Teresa who said, 'With God, there are no unwanted babies.'

God giving birth?

Now hear God speaking to Job in the final chapters of that puzzling book:

'Who shut in the sea with doors
when it burst out from the womb?—
when I made the clouds its garment,
and thick darkness its swaddling band,
and prescribed bounds for it,
and set bars and doors,
and said, "Thus far shall you come, and no farther,
and here shall your proud waves be stopped"? ...
Has the rain a father,
or who has begotten the drops of dew?
From whose womb did the ice come forth,
and who has given birth to the hoarfrost of heaven?'
(Job 38:8–11, 28–29)

This seems to suggest that God has not just created the world (and continues to nurture it) but that there is a sense in which God has 'birthed' the world. I'm not saying that God suffered pain in its creation or that God has a womb, but that there is an intimate, almost biological link between God and his/her created world. So God not only cares for each child in its mother's womb but is a sort of mother to all creation.

This may appear radical, but in fact there are clues throughout the Bible to the 'motherhood of God'. When the Bible talks of God's compassion and mercy, the Hebrew word most commonly used for compassion is directly related to the word for 'womb'. The Bible tells us repeatedly that God has 'womb-love' for us, God's children.

The concept of God as mother also comes up in Jesus' anguished cry to the people of Jerusalem:

Jerusalem, Jerusalem, the city that kills the prophets and stones those who are sent to it! How often have I desired to gather your children together as a hen gathers her brood under her wings, and you were not willing! (Luke 13:34)

The 14th-century hermit Julian of Norwich, in her *Revelations of Divine Love*, also known as *Showings*, talks at length of God as our mother, and especially of Jesus as our mother, both by nature and by grace, who has birthed us by the cross (although she continues to call him 'he'):

The mother's service is nearest, readiest and surest: nearest because it is most natural, readiest because it is most loving, and surest because it is truest. No one ever might or could perform this office fully, except only him. We know that all our mothers bear us for pain and for death… But our true Mother Jesus, he alone bears us for joy and for endless life, blessed may he be… This fair lovely word 'mother' is so sweet and so kind in itself that it cannot truly be said of anyone or to anyone except of him and to him who is the true Mother of life and of all things.[1]

Julian was a celibate hermit and never experienced motherhood herself. I think she must have had a very caring mother! Her image of Jesus as mother is not just from her imagination but has strong biblical roots. The Bible can be problematic for women who want to reflect on the meaning of their womanhood. Jesus, after all, never experienced menstruation, childbirth and menopause. How can we women find our lives reflected in the Bible and find God in our specifically female experiences? Perhaps one way we can do this is by searching for references to God's motherhood of us in the Bible. There are more than you think!

Agony and ecstasy

Well, the long-awaited day came, when the 'Braxton-Hicks contractions' (mild contractions that precede labour), turned into something more frequent and more painful. It was a Sunday, we had just been to church, and I rang the hospital and told them my symptoms. 'Oh no, you're not in labour yet,' they cheerfully pronounced, even though I was convinced my pains were frequent enough to warrant going in. After a certain amount of arguing, I put down the phone and declared that we were going in anyway. So I took up my pre-packed hospital bag, and Ed drove me to the hospital we had chosen. I had been to free assertiveness classes during my pregnancy and had got more assertive as my bump got bigger, and I was to find that assertiveness very useful throughout what ended up as two hospital stays.

Was I glad I had gone with my instinct! The moment I reached the hospital, I started bleeding, and they immediately whisked me into a pre-maternity emergency ward where they monitored me all night. By the morning I was ready for the labour ward, and the real work began. They say the way to make God laugh is to tell God your plans. I don't know about that, but if you show a midwife your 'birth plan', she must be very tempted to laugh. Things rarely go according to plan, and as an 'elderly primigravida' I was more vulnerable to problems in birth than a younger woman would be. I'm going to spare you all the details, as I'm sure you really don't want to know (especially if you are a male reader). Suffice it to say that my labour was difficult, very painful, and not remotely like the very 'natural' birth I had hoped for. The only light relief was that I took so much gas and air that I pronounced in the middle, 'I've been all the way from Derbe to Lystra'—we had thought about Paul's missionary journeys at church the day before!

At last my baby, dragged out of me by a very red-faced doctor with a forceps, was placed on my chest, along with the announcement, 'It's a boy!' Was there a flicker of disappointment that this was not the girl I had dreamt of having? I don't think so—I was just so glad that my baby was born. He was greyish and quiet, with a bruised face from the forceps, so he was whisked away at once for oxygen, and I fell into a much-needed sleep.

A couple of hours later, Ed woke me up and said, 'I think he's thirsty. His mouth is moving a lot.' So he placed the baby on my breast and, even though I was lying down, which is not the easiest way to breastfeed, little John latched on immediately. 'That's my boy,' I said spontaneously, and from that moment I knew he was all I wanted. I also got a better look at his face, and my first thought was 'Ed', which was just as well, really—not that there was ever any doubt who his father was!

Some women, I know, find it hard to bond with their infants, but I had no such trouble with John. In the midst of the chaos of the labour ward, I immediately felt a love deeper than any I had ever experienced, yet somehow familiar too. The Victorian poet Alice Meynell (1847–1922) wrote a poem, 'Maternity', about the mother of a stillborn child, ten years after its birth:

One wept whose only child was dead,
New-born, ten years ago.
'Weep not; he is in bliss,' they said.
She answered, 'Even so,

Ten years ago was born in pain
A child, not now forlorn.
But oh, ten years ago, in vain,
A mother, a mother was born.'

That was how I felt as John began to feed from me: 'A mother was born.'

Battles

What I didn't yet know was how many battles I would have to fight as a mother, not only immediately after his birth but throughout his life. The first battle was that the night nurse absolutely refused to permit for John to sleep in the bed with me, although he cried every time I put him in the plastic cot. Eventually, I was allowed to have him with me in bed, provided I put a sheet over both of us and tucked it in, which was pretty unwelcome in the summer heat. I didn't see how he could possibly roll out of bed as babies can't roll for three months, and I was convinced I would sleep lightly enough to stay aware of him and not roll on to him. On his first night I spent the whole time with my hand on him, and in my over-excited, half-asleep state I thought I felt another hand being gently laid on me, reassuring me. I still wonder about that.

As I was pretty knocked about, they kept me in hospital longer than normal, with Ed in almost constant attendance. On the fifth day, we gingerly left the maternity ward, with the baby in our car seat, and went home with great relief. But it wasn't to last long. The community midwife visited me the next morning and immediately said, 'You have to go to A&E.' Not only had my stitches come apart, and the wound looked infected, but she also spotted that I was dehydrated, which explained why the baby never seemed full after a breastfeed, and why we had to give him bottles as well. (I re-defined what doctors call the 'let-down reflex', as 'the feeling of disappointment you get when your baby has breastfed for an hour and still drinks a full bottle'.)

I was whisked back into hospital like a shot, this time on a general gynaecological ward as the maternity ward couldn't re-admit. So began what Ed called, 'Hell on the fifth floor'. At least I had a single room with en-suite bathroom, although, as I found out, this was not so much for my benefit as to keep my baby's crying from disturbing the other patients. At the start, I was connected up to a double drip, one of rehydration salts and one of antibiotics to treat the infection. Both attached to the frame of my bed, so I couldn't move more than a couple of feet. In the midst of this I was trying to feed and change a week-old baby. Eventually, they moved a zed-bed into the ward, so that Ed could stay overnight with me, and he got hospital meals by wearing a shirt similar to that worn by the orderlies and going into the staff canteen.

Home

Finally I was released, and we could go home and get to know our new baby. It was an intense, dramatic period in our lives. All my senses were heightened, and I lived and breathed 'baby'. John was my total focus, and I could not think of anything else—except sleep, of course, of which I thought constantly. Our traumatic hospital experience, as well as John's irregular sleeping habits, exhausted Ed and me when we had hardly begun, but this is not unusual with new parents. As I was still recovering from my 'injuries', I was unable to sit down properly for some months, so apart from breastfeeding, Ed was John's main carer for his first six months or so.

We did manage to leave the house occasionally, even taking John to our church weekend away (although for only one night). One thing I noticed early in John's life was that when I went out without him, leaving him in Ed's care, I would not only find myself lactating when I thought about my baby, but that I would also have strange 'pangs' in my abdomen, feeling something like the Braxton-Hicks contractions. It was as though my love for my child was something physical, tugging on my guts, keeping me focused on him even when he wasn't with me.

Does God, looking at us, God's children, feel similar darts of longing to be with us and for us to love God back? God's love is, after all, not a detached kind of general love, but a particular, emotional, parent-like love. Could God, too, feel those 'after-pangs', as God created us and in effect gave birth to us? This may sound too feminist to you, but bear in mind that one of the Bible's central images of how we can belong to God and know we are God's children is the image of birth. When Nicodemus wanted to know how he could follow Jesus, Jesus answered:

'Very truly, I tell you, no one can see the kingdom of God without being born from above.' Nicodemus said to him, 'How can anyone be born after having grown old? Can one enter a second time into the mother's womb and be born?' Jesus answered, 'Very truly, I tell you, no one can enter the kingdom of God without being born of water and Spirit. What is born of the flesh is flesh, and what is born of the Spirit is spirit. Do not be astonished that I said to you, "You must be born from above." The wind *blows where it chooses, and you hear the sound of it, but you do not know where it comes from or where it goes. So it is with everyone who is born of the Spirit.'* (John 3:3–8)

How is it that we have all learned parts of this by heart as the core of the gospel and failed to notice that Jesus, defining what it means to follow him, turns to women and women's experience for his chief metaphor? How has the church in its history marginalised, ignored or oppressed women, when women are so central to Jesus' teaching here?

Or listen to the epistle writer James talking about how we have been birthed by God:

Every generous act of giving, with every perfect gift, is from above, coming down from the Father of lights, with whom there is no variation or shadow due to change. In fulfilment of his own purpose he gave us birth by the word of truth, so that we would become a kind of first fruits of his creatures. (1:17–18)

I find this extraordinary: one moment God is 'the Father' and then in the very next verse, 'he' is giving birth. Therefore I don't think that it is too radical or too feminist to see God in the experience of birth—or indeed to see birth in the experience of God.

Loved from the first

I loved my son passionately as soon as I saw him properly, even though I had been all geared up for him to be a daughter. A baby is a bundle of love waiting to be expressed, and it is more than tragic when that love is not reciprocated. Likewise, God loves us from the start, perhaps as soon as

God thinks of creating us: 'He chose us in Christ before the foundation of the world' (Ephesians 1:4).

Just as I immediately recognised Ed in John (the mouth and eyes were unmistakable), so we human beings are made in the image of God, our father. I have already suggested that a central feature of our being made in God's image is our capacity to be in relationship to others and to communicate—in fact, to love. Animals have this ability to a limited extent but it is far more developed in humans, with our vastly increased use of language.

So we reflect God simply by being born in God's image; but if we belong to Jesus, we can come to reflect that image much more fully and experience the restoration of that image which has been partly lost through our fallenness. If we are following Jesus and walking in the Spirit, people should be able to see traces of God in our faces and in our words and behaviour.

The more my son grows up, I find, the more he is getting like his father in personality and mannerisms. Can the same be said of our parent–child relationship with God? As we grow to 'the measure of the full stature of Christ' (Ephesians 4:13), surely we come to look more and more like 'a chip off the old block'. (Jesus was a carpenter, so I feel free to use that workbench metaphor.)

A rather eccentric friend of mine with a faith prone to wobbles (but whose isn't?) once told me, 'I have worked out what God is up to with this world. God is in the process of reproducing himself.' I thought that was a very profound statement, not only about our creation, but also about our redemption.

In one sense we are children of God by our very nature. But because we and our world have been and continue to be damaged by sin, we need to be 're-adopted' into God's family by being 'born from above'. In fact, Paul frequently uses the language of adoption in his epistles, to express our status in Christ: 'When the fullness of time had come, God sent his Son, born of a woman, born under the law, in order to redeem those who were under the law, so that we might receive adoption as children' (Galatians 4:4–5).

These images of adoption, also found in Romans and Ephesians, could be a rich source of spiritual nourishment for adoptive parents, who have perhaps not been able to bring forth a child but who are in a sense in a 'God-like' position in relation to their children, having chosen them to bring up and love. I shall have more to say about this later.

Nourishment

Newborn babies need constant tender care and nourishment to survive. Likewise, God has prepared a world that has everything in it that God's creatures need to live. If just one factor in the makeup of our planet were different, it might not have arrived at the conditions for life. It's a miracle that we're here at all!

Nourishment was a sore point as far as my baby was concerned. He was big at birth (although he steadily moved down the growth charts) and very hungry. I didn't realise that the heat of the hospital was making me dehydrated, and so he wasn't getting enough milk. By the fourth day we were trying bottles, which we had sworn we wouldn't (there went the next plan…). Soon we were bottle-feeding him at night, and only breastfeeding by day, which was a mistake, as it didn't stimulate my milk enough, and eventually I had to give up.

One thing I noticed, however, was that after a bottle-feed, John would stop crying, and perhaps sleep, but after a breastfeed, he had a deeply satisfied expression on his face that just wasn't there after a bottle-feed. It seems we are fundamentally meant for relationship and human contact. The newborn baby gazes at its mother because she is the primary object in the baby's life, and because it is learning to focus. In the early days the baby begins to recognise its mother's features, voice and smell. This can't really be called love—it's more of a survival mechanism.

Nevertheless, all this, for the baby, is the first lesson in what love means. While this happens, the mother too is learning to know her own baby (and so is the father, although perhaps less intensely). While in hospital, I soon found that even through the earplugs I was wearing to help me sleep I could recognise my own baby's cry as he lay in his cot, and distinguish it from other babies'.

Just as my baby (and I) learned all these things at the start, so 'children of God' have to learn to recognise God's voice, God's features, even, one might say, the 'smell of God':

But thanks be to God, who in Christ always leads us in triumphal procession, and through us spreads in every place the fragrance that comes from knowing him. For we are the aroma of Christ to God among those who are being saved and among those who are perishing. (2 Corinthians 2:14–15)

Equally, as the baby learns to suck at the mother's breast, we, when we are first followers of Jesus, need to learn to feed on the Spirit. The baby's first experience of love is as milk; so our first experiences of God's love may be of God protecting us, showing us in everyday 'coincidences' that

God is present and caring for us. The baby learns love by responding to the mother's and father's love. As we respond to God's love of us, we begin to experience that love and find out what true love is. Later this intimate care may appear to lessen, for God's own reasons—but that is for a later chapter.

Only for you

Pregnancy and birth, as well as the subsequent child-rearing, bring out qualities in the parents that they didn't know they had. Before we had John, Ed was of the general opinion that many men have that all babies look alike and that small babies are basically boring until they start to walk and talk. As soon as he was a father, he began to discover how fascinating a small baby can be: his facial expressions, his responses to external stimuli, his beauty when asleep. (Ed used to call John 'Foetus Features' when he slept!)

I, too, having been single for a long time and having had no younger brothers or sisters, or even cousins, was afraid that I might not take naturally to being a mother. Yet as soon as I was one, I found myself remembering long forgotten nursery rhymes, automatically playing with my baby in ways I must have been played with myself as an infant, and feeling a deep, healing connection with my own birth and infancy.

I have already said that I don't think God *had* to create a world with human beings in it. I think it might be fair to say that in creating that world, God expressed qualities that could not have been expressed in any other way. When we— if we are able—make a choice to be parents, we are choosing to share the love we have for each other with a new human being.

Sometimes I see people in the street or on the bus who

have poverty and deprivation written all over them: not just homeless people begging, but people whose facial expression suggests that they have never known unconditional love, or whose body proclaims a lifetime of bad diet. When I see these people, I think, 'Once you were someone's perfect, beloved new baby.' Of course that may not be true, because so many babies are unwanted or unloved. What I should be thinking instead, perhaps, is, 'Once you were God's deeply loved new baby, and God has not stopped looking at you that way.' That is an amazing thought with which to end this chapter.

Chapter 3

Growth and learning

' 'Ello Dada'

'Change and decay in all around I see.' I've always disliked this line from the admittedly popular hymn 'Abide with me' (Henry Lyte, 1849), although the words become strangely more relevant as I grow older. Why equate change with decay? Why not 'Change and growth in all around I see'?

In becoming parents, we opt for a life of constant change. As soon as we have mastered one stage of a child's development, the child has moved on to another stage, and we have to start learning all over again. Just as I got the hang of feeding with milk, my son was ready to start on solids; just as we learned to cope with him 'cruising' around the room holding on to furniture, he started to walk hands-free. (Sadly I missed his first six steps as I was looking the other way at the time, while everyone else in the room saw him.) I once saw a cartoon of two parents with a crawling baby: the parents had suspended all their possessions, including their furniture, from hammocks near the ceiling. One parent was saying to the other, 'It's only for three or four years…'

At the time, we often can't wait for our baby to get to the next stage, given the demands on our time and attention that an infant makes. I read a poem once in which the poet describes herself and her friend 'waiting for our babies/to grow an hour older'.[1] That certainly describes my feelings at times when John was an infant. Being the mother of an infant (or the father, if he is the main carer) can be an incredibly slow, tedious and exhausting state, which seems to go on for ever—and then suddenly you look round and it's gone, and you have a toddler. How did that happen?

Yet infants, as Ed discovered to his surprise, can also be extraordinarily fascinating. When your baby isn't crying with colic or wanting a nappy change, just to sit and gaze into its eyes as it gazes into yours is perhaps one of the most 'worshipful' experiences we can have—a mutual 'worship', or honouring, between the parent and child. Does God, too, enjoy it when we gaze into God's eyes, in communal worship or personal prayer? I think so, but in the same way that we also want our child to begin to explore the world around it, God wants us to explore this world God has given us, and to find ways to serve God and others in it.

As far as physical development and exploring the world goes, John reached many of his 'milestones' quite early. Yet he never behaved quite like other babies. He was more demanding, more active, more alert. Other parents were putting their infants to bed at 6 p.m. or 7 p.m. and having an evening to relax before an interrupted night. Our baby refused ever to sleep before 8.30 p.m. or 9 p.m., by which time it was too late to enjoy a film or TV programme. Usually I was quite ready for bed myself by the time we had 'got him down'.

The most astounding thing happened when he was a mere five and a half months old. He was awake (as often) in the middle of the night, and Ed said to me, 'I think he's swinging the lead' (in other words, trying to get away with staying awake). Imagine our surprise when John said, quite clearly, 'Ding led.' A few weeks later, Ed said directly to John, 'Say "Hello Daddy",' and John replied instantly, 'Ello Dada.' It was like being in that film *Look Who's Talking*, in which Bruce Willis plays the voice of the baby. It was also at five months or so that John made his first 'joke', as I was dressing him in his Babygro™. He pulled the Babygro over his face and then pulled it off again and burst into fits of giggles. He had learned to play 'peep-bo' with me!

C.S. Lewis describes in one of his books that when we pray it is a bit like fishing: we have our 'line' stretched out to God, and suddenly there is movement on the other end of it. 'It's alive!' we exclaim. Nurturing a baby is very like that too: you think at first the communication is all one way, and then suddenly your baby takes the initiative and 'talks' back to you, and you realise you have a separate, thinking being on your hands. It's one of the most exciting moments in the world. I wonder if God feels similarly excited when we make our first prayer, our first response to the God who has always been communicating with us.

Proud

Of course every new baby is the cleverest in the world! We were convinced that John's sleeplessness was entirely due to his high intelligence. We all feel inordinate pride as our child learns new skills and ways of relating to objects and people, moving from babble to talk, to reading, to writing; learning to move a swing independently, or to ride a bike. Does God, too, feel pride in God's children as they toddle into the kingdom and slowly but surely learn to walk in the light? I think perhaps God does. More than that, I think God takes pride in the whole world, in all human beings, whether they have chosen to follow God or not. I imagine God watching the human race, as it grows from inarticulate sounds to language, from primitive social roles to a developed society, from stone tools to advanced technology, and beaming with pride at all that these children made in God's image have discovered and created. I picture God saying to himself, 'I can't wait until they find out about electricity…'

I wonder if, just as we parents are overjoyed to receive a drawing of a rough circle and four sticks with the words, 'This is you, Mummy,' so God is delighted when we present to God our very small, very imperfect offerings of worship and service. The baby's concept of its parents as separate beings is very basic at first, but—if development is normal—it slowly grows to recognise its parents as individuals like itself, with their own feelings, ideas and plans (plans that will no doubt have to be changed as a result of having that baby!). So as we come to God, whether as children or later in life, we begin like infants, understanding very little of God's nature or of what God wants, and gradually we learn to listen to God, to hear God's call and to obey it.

An anonymous post on the Ship of Fools website (www. ship-of-fools.com) put it like this:

I think of praying and learning to pray much as a baby learns to speak. As a parent, I got very good at knowing what my (as yet) speechless children wanted and needed, but that didn't stop me slowly teaching them to speak, ask and say 'please' when they did ask.

Perhaps 'praying in tongues' is actually a kind of baby babble in which we can speak to God when we have no other language to express our feelings? I certainly find it's my first resort in times of crisis, when I can't spare the time or energy to utter a well set-out prayer. God listens even when our prayers are incoherent and when perhaps all we can do is utter a cry of 'Help!' or speak the name of the person for whom we're praying.

Just a parent learns to interpret 'Goo-goo' (or even 'ding led'!), so God interprets our inarticulate prayers and groans when we hardly know what to pray for:

Likewise the Spirit helps us in our weakness; for we do not know how to pray as we ought, but that very Spirit intercedes with sighs too deep for words. And God, who searches the heart, knows what is the mind of the Spirit, because the Spirit intercedes for the saints according to the will of God. (Romans 8:26–27)

Nevertheless, just as the parent is thrilled when the baby can actually tell you what it wants, so God wants us to grow more articulate in our prayers, to learn to speak to God, and to understand the answer. The baby learns first how to relate to its parent, and then gradually (if development is proceeding normally) to relate socially to others and to live in harmony with them. As we learn to speak and listen to God, so we are also learning how best to communicate with our brothers and sisters in God and, in fact, with everyone we encounter.

Growing up

Recently I watched a toddler on the bus handing his mother one of those wrapped straws from a small carton of juice. She obligingly took off the wrapper for him, and he took back the straw and turned it thoughtfully in his hands. Without any words, they understood each other perfectly. Next I saw her give him a little clockwork toy that would spin round if you wound up its feet. The mother had already wound it up, so the boy watched it spin once, holding it upside down and letting its feet spin instead of its body. The next thing was fascinating: the boy, with his tiny fingers, attempted to wind it up again. He managed only one turn, so the toy span only marginally, but he was clearly getting the idea. He was learning through the toy how to manipulate objects, how to find out how things work, how to coordinate his eyes and his fingers.

As our children grow, we take pleasure in their growing independence. One of my son's first 'sentences', when he was still under two, was, 'I do it a self,' which he repeated several times a day! We, if we are parenting well, welcome our children's ability to 'do it a self'. Yet as Christians, we have often talked as if we are to remain in perpetual infancy in our relationship with God. You may be old enough to remember the infamous 'Children of God' or 'Family of Love' cult, started in the late 1960s, with their catchy chorus, 'You gotta be a baby'. Surely God, if God is a good parent, wants us to learn to care for ourselves, not to mention for others.

I heard a speaker at my university say, 'When you leave college, go and sit under the best ministry you can find.' Is that the role of a congregation—to sit and be spoon-fed with the right answers by the clergy? I believe that the writer of Ephesians means it when he says that we are to build up the body of Christ 'until all of us come to the unity of the faith and of the knowledge of the Son of God, to maturity, to the measure of the full stature of Christ' (Ephesians 4:13). When we are new Christians, infants in the kingdom of God, Paul tells the Corinthians we need easily digestible milk:

And so, brothers and sisters, I could not speak to you as spiritual people, but rather as people of the flesh, as infants in Christ. I fed

you with milk, not solid food, for you were not ready for solid food.
(1 Corinthians 3:1–2)

We find a similar thought in Hebrews, as the writer rebukes his audience:

You need milk, not solid food; for everyone who lives on milk, being still an infant, is unskilled in the word of righteousness. But solid food is for the mature, for those whose faculties have been trained by practice to distinguish good from evil. (5:12–14)

A new Christian is a 'spiritual baby' and needs extra care and spiritual feeding. But God doesn't want us to stay babies for ever: God teaches us to crawl, to toddle and then to walk in the light of Christ. That means churches need to provide appropriate spiritual food for both those who are just crawling in the light, and those who feel ready to learn to run.

We are not meant to stop at milk; we are meant to grow into eating solids—that's what our teeth are for! (I do know mothers who have breastfed until their child is the age of five, and maybe that does have psychological advantages, but even these mothers didn't keep their children exclusively on milk after six months or so.)

I love Hosea's picture of God parenting the toddler Israel:

When Israel was a child, I loved him,
and out of Egypt I called my son…
Yet it was I who taught Ephraim to walk,
I took them up in my arms;
but they did not know that I healed them.
I led them with cords of human kindness,
with bands of love.

I was to them like those
who lift infants to their cheeks.
I bent down to them and fed them (Hosea 11:1, 3–4)

This must be the only mention of toddler equipment (leading reins) in the Bible! It is a lovely image of how God helps us to move on in our faith, to learn to stand and set out on the first steps of discipleship.

There is, of course, a sense in which we are always going to be dependent on God, as God guides us by the Spirit through our daily lives. But we are not meant to stay babies in the kingdom, or to be always dependent on Christian teachers for our thinking and actions. We are meant to be able to work out God's will for ourselves—not just as individuals but together as the body of Christ. God, as a good parent, will certainly respond to our 'I do it a self' by letting us have a go.

I worry when I hear preachers exhorting people to go back to the time when they first became Christians and to remember how enthusiastic they were then. It sounds a bit like a couple staying in a perpetual honeymoon. Thinking back to how our love was then may be a way to put new spark into our marriage, but we should also be able to accept that a marriage 'grows up' and reaches a different quality of relationship than it had at the first—and that this is not a decline but a maturing. The same goes for our faith. A Christian who still has exactly the same doctrinal and ethical opinions at 50 as she had at 20 is not necessarily someone who has been exceptionally faithful to God. She may be someone who has got stuck and ossified.

Still a child

A couple of years after 'I do it a self', I watched in amazement as John taught himself to read at the age of three. He had been bashing away on computers practically from the time he could sit up. We had a programme called 'Baby Smash', in which a baby could hit any key (or several keys at once!) and interesting shapes and colours would come up on the screen, with accompanying sounds. As a result of this computer exposure, the first few words he could read were 'Yes', 'No', 'Enter', 'Exit', 'Quit' and 'Cancel' (not to mention 'Tesco', 'Ikea' and 'Barnet'). By the age of four, when he started school, he could read fluently, and the Reception teacher had to go upstairs and fetch books for him from Year One, as the Reception books were far too easy for him.

Yet it would still be many years before he stopped wanting me to read to him at night—not only because it was less work for him, but because that was a special time for him and me, or him and his father. My parents went on reading to me (sometimes in German, which I couldn't read but could understand) long after I became an independent reader.

Similarly, there is no point at which we no longer need God to lead and care for us. Our children never stop being our children, no matter how independent! Nor do we stop being our parents' children. (I have mixed feelings about this as my mother, who is 96, still tries sometimes to run my life...)

So, I'm not saying that we ever 'grow away' from God and become totally independent. Actually, none of us is totally independent of each other anyway—human beings are meant to be interdependent. What I am saying is that when we are children in the faith, we relate to God as children, and once we are adults we should be relating to God as adults, not expecting to be dictated to every day as to whether we should go this way or that. We will still need to hear God's voice guiding us, but it may not be as clear and as specific as it was when we first became Christians. After a few years of parenting, a parent expects a child to do what is right and avoid what is wrong, not by the parent's spelling it out every time (which would be very wearing) but by the child's having internalised the voice of the parent and making the right choices for itself. So, too, the Spirit of God lives within us and we are expected to be able to make decisions by that Spirit, without having any obvious 'signs' or voices from on high.

Weaned but worshipping

What does it mean, both to be able to make our own decisions, and to rely on God to guide us? To be still dependent on God but not infantile? I think it may be something like Psalm 131:

O Lord, my heart is not lifted up,
my eyes are not raised too high;
I do not occupy myself with things
too great and too marvellous for me.
But I have calmed and quieted my soul,
like a weaned child with its mother;
my soul is like the weaned child that is with me.
O Israel, hope in the Lord
from this time on and forevermore.

For years I read this psalm as a picture of a tiny infant, sleeping on its mother's breast, perhaps after a feed. Then I suddenly noticed the adjective 'weaned'. This is not a child who needs to suck at its mother's breast any more: this is a child who has begun to eat solid food, perhaps even a child that can already feed itself with a spoon—therefore a child who has begun to be a bit independent of the mother. Yet the child still wants to rest on its mother's bosom, absorbing mother-love and acceptance. I think this says something about our need for God, which continues to be great, whatever our own level of competence. We are meant to be adults, but adults who are not too embarrassed to hug their family or friends, and adults who can go to God, without shame, for spiritual nourishment.

By the way, this psalm speaks of a mother; but the fact that it is a weaned child, no longer dependent on the breast, suggests that it could equally be a father cuddling a toddler. I applaud the fact that nowadays fathers take a much more 'hands on' approach to fatherhood. It is no longer unusual, at least where I live, to see a father pushing a buggy along the pavement or attending a toddler group (which can, however, still be an intimidating place for men!). This change in society makes us perhaps in a better position to understand the 'motherly father' that I believe God to be to us.

Worship or service?

I want to say something more here about worship. I've described the baby's gaze as it rests in the parent's arms as a kind of worship. It strikes me that when we say a child 'worships' one or both parents, this is not always a positive thing. I know a woman who 'worshipped' her father, and she has never really got over his death. A parent who wanted her children to worship her would probably not be a good parent! What kind of parent wants this kind of adulation from his child?

I've heard it said that God desires our worship, but I'm really not that sure. Of course, worshipping God is different from worshipping a human parent, because God is perfect and humans are not. God is also holy and wholly different from us, so God is worthy of our worship. Nevertheless, I don't see much enthusiasm from the God of the Bible for religious services. Take this from Amos, speaking on behalf of God:

I hate, I despise your festivals,
and I take no delight in your solemn assemblies.
Even though you offer me your burnt offerings and grain offerings,
I will not accept them;
and the offerings of well-being of your fatted animals
I will not look upon.
Take away from me the noise of your songs;
I will not listen to the melody of your harps.
But let justice roll down like waters,
and righteousness like an ever-flowing stream. (5:21–28)

Several other passages in the prophets contain the same thought. It sounds as if God is much keener on our doing God's will, pursuing justice in the world, than on our singing a charismatic chorus five times or repeating the litany for Good Friday! Here is a similar thought from Hebrews 10:5–7, where the writer speaks for Christ, quoting Psalm 40:6–8:

Sacrifices and offerings you have not desired,
but a body you have prepared for me;
in burnt offerings and sin offerings
you have taken no pleasure.
Then I said, 'See, God, I have come to do your will, O God.'

Of course a parent wants a child to say, 'I love you' back, and our hymn-singing and prayers are a way of declaring that to God. But I can't help thinking that God's chief desire is not for what we do on a Sunday morning but for us to do God's will and serve God's kingdom from Monday to Saturday. This is borne out by Paul, who wrote in Romans, 'I appeal to you therefore, brothers and sisters, by the mercies of God, to present your bodies as a living sacrifice, holy and acceptable to God, which is your spiritual worship' (12:1). Here, Paul effectively says that what we do in our daily lives, in service of God, is worship. The only way to be a living sacrifice is to live.

I think this has a parallel in parenthood too. We want our children to love us, but most of all we want them to grow up as people with values we assent to, people who will love and serve God, people who will contribute to the world. God has the very same wish for us.

As for what we usually call worship, I think it is a way of feeling connected with God, a cuddle with God, if we may put it that way—but I also think that most of what goes on on a Sunday morning is for our benefit. By bringing before our hearts and minds the character and deeds of God, we learn to reflect God in our daily lives, just as a child, as it grows, learns its values and behaviour not just from what its parents say, but what it sees them doing and living out.

Pink or blue?

At the risk of sounding like the TV detective Columbo, there's one more thing I'd like to talk about in this chapter...

Often on the bus or in the street I stop to admire someone else's baby. (I have even found myself accidentally talking to a TV star who lives near us as a result!) I can nearly always tell if it's a boy or a girl, even if it's quite tiny—not by looking at the face, although some babies do have a very girlish or boyish face, but by checking out its clothes. You can be reasonably sure that if a baby is dressed in pink, it's going to be a girl, although with more neutral colours, you can't always tell.

One of the things our children are learning almost from the pushchair onwards is how to be a boy or a girl. Experiments have shown that when young people are given a baby to hold and play with, they will play more roughly with it if they have been told it's a boy than if they have been told it's a girl. Right from the very start we are socialising our kids into what we consider appropriate gender roles. Shops advertise 'boys' toys' and 'girls' toys' even for quite small children. Girls' clothes come in all sorts of attractive colours, whereas it's almost impossible to get boys' clothes in anything but blue, green, grey or shades of brown. A worrying number of boys' clothes come in variations of military camouflage, which is very frustrating for a pacifist like me. Are we training our boys from toddlerhood to be fighters?

Some of us dissent from strict gender roles and try to leave it open for our kids to be whoever they want to be, not conformed to what the world thinks is masculine or feminine. Yet still somehow our boys choose trucks and fire engines to play with, and our girls go straight for the Barbie™ dolls. Is there something innate and genetically determined here, or are very small children just absorbing these differences from the society around them without knowing it?

I personally think it's probably a bit of both. We know more now about the interactions of genes and environment, and we have the science of 'epigenetics', which explores how certain genes are switched on or off by the environment. Our children may be predetermined to be 'girlish' or 'boyish' but how we treat them, and what kind of role models we give them, reinforces those differences and perhaps exaggerates them beyond what they would naturally be. In my childhood I can't remember being all that wedded to pink—in fact I was a tomboy and preferred scrambling round in a sweater and tough trousers. I can still remember the acute disappointment I felt one Christmas when I had asked for a Robin Hood outfit—and my mother had scoured the shops searching for a Maid Marian outfit, with a skirt. I didn't want to be Maid Marian, staying at camp, cooking venison; I wanted to be Robin, going out into the forest and having adventures! Everywhere you go, at every supermarket and every theme park, pink fairy dresses are being pushed at girls and 'hero' outfits at boys.

Does this matter? I think it does. It matters not just because of the large minority who don't fit the stereotypes, or the small group who are brought up as one sex when they feel profoundly that they are the other. It matters because it limits people's lives and discourages them from using their unique talents. It matters because, however equal a society we proclaim ourselves to be, boys still get steered into boys' jobs and girls into girls' jobs. And girls' jobs are still paid roughly 25 per cent less than boys' jobs. Look at the average board of directors of a big company. I can guarantee you that it will have no more than one or two women on it (and probably no ethnic minorities at all). Even if women are by nature more geared to the personal and relational, surely those are the very qualities that we need in order to change our often greedy and competitive business culture.

Of course, things have changed a great deal for the better

in the last century. Nevertheless, it is hard to break out of the mindset of gender-based judgments like 'big boys don't cry', which has done such psychological damage to so many—and which affects adult relationships between men and women when men are unable to show or speak their feelings.

Traditional

Unfortunately, when it came to modelling a role for John, Ed and I have found we have a very traditional division of labour in our house. We have settled into the household jobs that we know how to do and have been brought up to do: he mows the lawn, empties the bin and fixes any car problems, while I do all the laundry, most of the cooking and deciding what goes where in the house. It seems it's not so easy to depart from what we saw our mothers and fathers doing!

Nevertheless, Ed does do an increasing amount of cooking, and occasionally a bit of vacuuming (when the cleaner hasn't come). I hope we have never said anything to John that implies that boys must do or can't do certain things. Yet still he feels embarrassed by having bought a pair of pink headphones for his iPod (they were in the sale) and refuses to wear socks that have even a tiny, invisible bit of pink in them. Where does he get it from?

What about the church? Sadly, many churches appear still to be living in the 19th century, not even in the 20th, when it comes to issues like women's leadership or women's preaching. Mine is not one of them, which is one of the reasons why I'm there. Sometimes, when leading worship in our congregation, we have to make a special effort to make sure some men are involved!

What does God think of all this? Some conservative Christians believe that it is God's will that we should be socialised into clear and different gender roles. They might even say these are built into our very nature. (If that's so, why do these people get so frightened that these 'innate' roles will be destroyed the minute we let a woman lead the service? Surely something that's built into our nature can't be so easily erased?) However, if God is a parent who loves every child infinitely, why would God be so affected by what sex the child is? When John was born, I was overjoyed despite my deep wish for a girl. I really didn't care what sex he was: he was a healthy baby with nothing missing, and that was all that mattered. Won't God feel the same about every infant born into this world and long for that individual to reach their full potential as a human being rather than fulfilling a preordained role?

The early Christians amazed the people of their society by rescuing babies that had been left abandoned on hillsides to die. These were sometimes babies with disabilities, who might have died anyway, given the minimal medical knowledge of the time (but they could have died in loving arms, not alone on a hillside...). However, the vast majority were simply female infants and the parents had wanted a son. By rescuing them and adopting them, the first Christians were saying that God values every human being born on this planet, regardless of what sex they are. Female infanticide, or abortion when the parents have found out they are having a girl, still persists in some countries to this day—although both are almost always illegal. They do not happen in cultures that have been formed by Christianity.

I believe God is very much less concerned about gender roles than many of God's followers are. There are many instances in the Bible of people being called by God to do things that break out of their gender roles: at least one female prophet (Deborah, in Judges 4—5); a female interpreter of scripture (Huldah, in 2 Kings 22:14–20); a woman, Mary Magdalene, who is chosen as the first witness to the resurrection of Jesus (John 20), even though a woman's testimony was not valid in court; men doing 'women's work', like the water carrier who leads the disciples to the Upper Room (Mark 14 and Luke 22).

Circumcision, the Old Testament sign of belonging to God's people, could be performed only on men (ancient Israel did not have the horrific practice sometimes called 'female circumcision' still practised in parts of the world today). A woman belonged to God's people by virtue of belonging to a man who did. The new covenant uses baptism as the sign of joining God's people, and this is a sign that can be performed on both men and women equally. It is the context of talking about baptism that Paul makes his great statement of sexual, ethnic and economic equality:

As many of you as were baptised into Christ have clothed your-selves with Christ. There is no longer Jew or Greek, there is no longer slave or free, there is no longer male and female; for all of you are one in Christ Jesus. And if you belong to Christ, then you are Abraham's offspring, heirs according to the promise.
(Galatians 3:27–29)

Bishop Graham Cray gave a talk many years ago based on these verses, in which he said that this verse set off three time bombs for change. The first—Jews and Greeks—went off immediately, when Peter had his vision, which resulted in his going and baptising Cornelius and his household (the story is in Acts 10). The second, the relationship between slave and free, took another 1800 years to go off, with the anti-slavery movement led largely by Christians. The third, the relationship between men and women, is going off in the church right now (although it went off in society much earlier), and the resultant fall-out is a source of pain to many on both sides of the argument. To my mind, and that of many others, including many biblical scholars, these verses undeniably tell us that traditional gender distinctions no longer matter in Christ. Does God really think girls can't be engineers or boys can't wear pink? I very much doubt it.

Chapter 4

Tears, tumbles and tantrums

A tumble

My parents were refugees from Austria, and I had been going there on holiday since I was four. It seemed a good idea to take our first Austrian holiday with John when he was four. We felt the need for a real rest, especially as I had recently taken him out of his Reception class because he had been having a very difficult time. We chose a remote spot in the mountains, far from any village or town and with a hotel that provided lots of children's activities, including an indoor pool and a large swimming pond.

Ed was getting John showered for bed when I heard crying and a shout of alarm. I rushed to the shower to find blood leaking copiously from John's chin. The shower had a tiled step leading down to it, and John had slipped in the wet and cut his chin open on the edge of the step. Panic all round ensued, especially from John!

Fortunately, it was the second week of the holiday, when we had hired a car to explore further afield. John was quickly patched up by hotel staff, with a sterile pad on his chin held on with gauze tied round the top of his head. He looked like one of those classic cartoons about toothache! Then we drove the 30 kilometres to the nearest hospital, with our E111 European medical treatment forms. When we got there, I was deeply impressed: although the lights were down, as it was now 9.30 p.m., we had only to show John's form and were almost immediately admitted to see the doctor, who gave him a few stitches. The hospital was modern, attractive and immaculately clean.

I'm telling this story not to criticise the NHS (from which, as I've said, I have had much wonderful treatment) or to praise Austria, but because that was one of those moments that brought out the depths of my love for my little son. I would have done almost anything to get him calmed down and fixed up. His need and upset called out both my and Ed's parental feelings in a way nothing but a crisis could. It seems that, in the times when our children are hurt, alone or in need, we love them even more than we previously thought possible. Does it work the same way with God? Does God love us, if such a thing were possible, even more when we are in pain?

More love

The other times when I found myself loving John most was when he did what we call 'throwing a wobbly'. To our surprise he did not have the dreaded 'terrible twos' that most parents expect and experience; at two years old he was still quite compliant and even-tempered. This I put down (wrongly, it turned out) to our having an exceptionally good child, or to the fact that we tried not to thwart him unnecessarily. The tantrums certainly came along later, and boy, did they come along! I would learn later to call them meltdowns, and also why he was having such bad ones.

I wish I could remember what it was that so often provoked his extreme distress and frustration when he was a small child, but then perhaps that is the merciful way the memory works. I have vivid memories of rows with my mother when

I was a child, which often ended in my running out of our house and down to the nearby railway line. (I used to find standing on the footbridge looking over the tracks peculiarly calming.) But I cannot for the life of me remember what a single row was about!

When John got in a state and was really distraught, he used to have a habit of repeating, 'Dee dee dee dee dee' in a most pathetic way. Nothing was so guaranteed to wrench my heartstrings than that little vocal utterance, which seemed to say, 'I am so upset that I can't get my words out, but I still need to tell you how upset I am.' I am ashamed to say that in his early years, Ed and I sometimes smacked John in an effort to calm him down. (It had worked very well on me once when I had hysterics as a child and my normally very patient father smacked me—the only time I can remember his ever hitting me.) Later we regretted our use of our greater strength and learned different, non-violent ways to deal with his outbursts. Even when he was small, though, I could never have smacked him when he was going, 'Dee dee dee.' I knew that what he needed then was the comfort of parental arms around him.

For many of us, there have been times in our lives when all we could come out with was incoherent noises. I remember that, when our dog was killed by a neighbour's car in our street only months after my brother had committed suicide, my mother went outside and started tearing leaves off a magnolia tree. It was the only way she could express her distress, which was of course much more grief for my brother than for the dog. It struck me as a particularly Jewish thing to do (my mother is Jewish); even today orthodox Jews tear the lapel of their jacket when someone dies, as a reminder of the 'rending of garments' that expressed sorrow in biblical times.

We saw in the last chapter that, just as a parent learns to understand what a baby wants even before it can form a single word, God listens to the incoherent groans of our hearts and can interpret what we mean and what we need.

It seems to me that often, when we are feeling down or distressed, or when we have done something of which we feel ashamed, we tend to hide from God, thinking God will not want to have anything to do with us in this state. Surely, far from running from God in shame in these times of disgrace, disappointment or depression, we should be most eager to run to God for consolation at these very times.

The culture in some churches does not help. Sometimes leaders teach us that God blesses us only when we are faithful. Accordingly, when bad things happen to us, we assume that we must have done something wrong and that we cannot approach the holy God until we have sorted ourselves out. I'm not talking here just about churches where the full (and false) 'prosperity gospel' is taught, but ordinary churches or Christian publications that tell us things like, 'God is so holy that he cannot look on sin.' (Why exactly does God always 'look on' things, not at them?) Well, apart from my innate suspicion about any statement that begins with, 'God cannot', I think this is theological nonsense.

If we were to say that 'God is so holy that we cannot look at God', there would be some biblical justification, for instance in Isaiah's life-changing vision of God:

And I said: 'Woe is me! I am lost, for I am a man of unclean lips, and I live among a people of unclean lips; yet my eyes have seen the King, the Lord of hosts!' Then one of the seraphs flew to me, holding a live coal that had been taken from the altar with a pair of tongs. The seraph touched my mouth with it and said: 'Now

that this has touched your lips, your guilt has departed and your
sin is blotted out.' (6:5–7)

If God cannot look at our sin, how on earth could Jesus have become incarnate and spent most of his time, not praying in the temple, but mixing with the 'dregs of society'? If this were true, we would have to be 100 per cent sinless before we even pray. I don't know about you, but I would never dare to pray at all. I suspect this thinking stems from a view of God as a kind of disapproving schoolmaster who punishes the slightest rule infringement harshly for the sake of the school in general. Is that really the God we meet in Jesus?

Falling

Sin and suffering are different from each other, of course— but they can have the same effect on us of making us wonder where God is in all this. They can also feel like each other: suffering in our lives can make us feel as though we must have done something wrong, and sin can feel like something we fell into accidentally, without meaning to. Haven't we all had moments when we said or did something that made us want to be swallowed by the floor? 'I didn't mean to say that, it just came out.'

Here I go back again to one of my favourite writers, Julian of Norwich. We have already seen how she describes Jesus as mother, but she also extends this image to cover different aspects of our life in Christ. Here she is talking about times of 'falling':

But often when our falling and our wretchedness are shown to us, we are so much afraid and so greatly ashamed of ourselves that we scarcely know where we can put ourselves. But then our courteous Mother does not wish us to flee away, for nothing would be less pleasing to him; but he then wants us to behave like a child. For when it is distressed and frightened, it runs quickly to its mother; and if it can do no more, it calls to the mother for help with all its might. So he wants us to act as a meek child, saying: My kind Mother, my gracious Mother, my beloved Mother, have mercy on me. I have made myself filthy and unlike you, and I may not and cannot make it right except with your help and grace.[1]

In many families (though not in all), the mother is the one who consoles and the father the one who disciplines. Not easy for the single parent who has to do both! But I do not think Julian of Norwich is portraying a God/mother who says, 'Wait until your father gets home.' I have heard the Second Coming preached about in a way that seems to say, 'He let you off in his first coming, but boy is he going to be angry when he comes again!' I don't think there is any biblical justification for this. In fact, Jesus tells us explicitly in John that his role is not to judge:

I do not judge anyone who hears my words and does not keep them, for I came not to judge the world, but to save the world. The one who rejects me and does not receive my word has a judge; on the last day the word that I have spoken will serve as judge. (12:47–48)

The world will be judged, but God's judgment is not one of condemnation. God's judgment has to be at least as fair and as loving as that of a good parent disciplining a child. Whether we have fallen into sin, or life has brought us unexpected distress, we can run to our God who loves us far more than any human mother could.

The lord and the servant

In the middle of Julian's revelations, she tells at some length of a vision she saw of a lord and a servant.[2] The lord is sitting on a throne, robed in majestic garments, looking with undiluted love at his servant below. The servant, dressed in short, dirty work clothes, has rushed off to do an errand for his lord and immediately fallen into a deep pit. He is bruised and wounded from his fall, and unable to get out of the pit by himself. What distresses him most is that he is unable to turn his head to see his master. So he doesn't know that, all the time, his lord is looking at him, not with anger at his fall but with deep love.

Julian interprets this vision on two levels. The lord is of course God. At one level the servant is Adam, or the archetypal human being, who has fallen into sin and is unable to rescue himself. At another level, the servant is Christ, who 'fell' into Mary's womb and was incarnated in the 'dirty work clothes' of our human flesh. In both cases the servant is unable to see clearly the glory and love of the father, for Adam is too damaged, and Jesus has chosen to live within the limits of being human. In both cases, the lord continues to beam at the servant, who he knows has fallen only in his eagerness to serve his Lord. Julian does not distinguish between sin and suffering here: they are both things which cause us to 'fall'. Jesus' suffering identifies him both with our suffering and with our sin. The cross is not only about 'crucifying' our sin but about healing our sufferings:

Surely he has borne our infirmities
and carried our diseases;
yet we accounted him stricken,
struck down by God, and afflicted.
But he was wounded for our transgressions,
crushed for our iniquities;
upon him was the punishment that made us whole,
and by his bruises we are healed. (Isaiah 53:4–5)

Julian's vision of the lord and the servant seems to me a profound parable of how God relates to us as God's children. From our limited human viewpoint, we tend to think that our fallibility somehow makes God love us less, and that God can love us only if we believe the right things and behave in the right way. Or we talk as if God loves Christians and hates everybody else. Actually:

God so loved the world that he gave his only Son, so that everyone who believes in him may not perish but may have eternal life. Indeed, God did not send the Son into the world to condemn the world, but in order that the world might be saved through him. (John 3:16–17, my emphasis)

Not everyone will respond, at least in this life, to the call of Jesus, but God's default position is love not only for the whole of humanity but for the whole of creation. We have been taught about God's being omnipresent (present everywhere), omniscient (all-knowing) and omnipotent (all-powerful) but how often do we hear of God being 'omniamorous'—all-loving? That's why I love Julian of Norwich's writings so much, because she speaks of God's 'omniamorousness'.

I worry a lot when I hear expressions of faith that are too

'other-worldly' and focus on rejecting this world and longing for the next. This world is fallen, flawed and full of selfishness and corruption. Even nature has turned into a battleground for survival: 'red in tooth and claw', as Tennyson put it.[3] But this is still the world that God made, and with which, Genesis tells us, God is very pleased (or 'well pleased', as a Cockney might say).

Why suffering?

If God is such a loving parent, why does God let us experience pain in the first place? Just imagine for a moment a child born without the ability to feel pain (although it is very rare, this does occur). What would happen if the child touched a hot electric cooker ring or cut itself with a knife? It would feel nothing and would not have the instinct to withdraw its hand immediately or run for help. Without pain receptors, we could not live at all in a world of dangers. This is the situation of people with Hansen's disease, or leprosy. Leprosy does not in itself cause injuries like the loss of fingers; rather, the disease destroys the nerves that feel pain, and this makes people with this disease injure themselves, often losing parts of their hands and feet which are the most exposed to danger.

I think the same is true emotionally and spiritually—when we feel pain in the depths of ourselves, it is a God-given sign that something is wrong and that we need to find a way to make it better. Psychiatrist M. Scott Peck talks in his book *The Road Less Travelled*[4] about the essential healthiness of depression: being depressed is a useful sign that there is something wrong in our lives and that we need to address it. This is a healthy psychological mechanism that a loving God has placed within us.

A good parent will want to keep his child away from pain, physical or psychological, as much as possible. But a parent who over-protects his child, who tries to keep it from any kind of suffering, is raising a child who will not develop the ability to face the dangers and trials of life. This is not actually a favour to the child. Equally, God might want to protect us from everything that could harm us, but God also wants us to grow into people who have the capacity to keep following during hard times—and sadly, the best way we can develop into that sort of people in this world is through hardship.

An angry God?

Then what about the wrath of God against sin? Christians, especially the more conservative sort, speak often about God's anger, and indeed this is a concept found in the Bible: 'For the wrath of God is revealed from heaven against all ungodliness and wickedness of those who by their wickedness suppress the truth' (Romans 1:18). Verses like this used to be employed a lot in evangelism. (I hope things have changed.) It's difficult to see how quoting this verse is supposed to attract people to love God and follow Jesus.

From my reading of the Old and New Testaments, I don't see the wrath of God, as it is often portrayed, as a kind of detached disapproval, in which God turns away from us in disgust. I see it rather more like the anger expressed by a mother whose child has been lost in a crowded place and just been found again. I've seen it again and again, and even done it myself: the moment your lost child is found, you burst out furiously, 'Where on earth have you been?' It's not that we're really angry with our child—it's just that the panicky emotions of having lost the child have to be expressed somehow, and they come out as anger. Of course, immediately after her outburst, the good mother (or father) immediately embraces the child and showers it with loving kisses.

I wonder whether God's anger is not a lot more like this: an emotional, involved anger at how things have gone wrong in the world. We ourselves get roused to anger by injustice in the world—must not God's anger at injustice be even greater? When I think of God's anger, I picture a mother who has just lost and re-found her child and is swooping down on it in relief:

I love you, O Lord, my strength.
The Lord is my rock, my fortress, and my deliverer,
my God, my rock in whom I take refuge...
In my distress I called upon the Lord;
to my God I cried for help.
From his temple he heard my voice,
and my cry to him reached his ears.
Then the earth reeled and rocked;
the foundations also of the mountains trembled
and quaked, because he was angry.
Smoke went up from his nostrils,
and devouring fire from his mouth;
glowing coals flamed forth from him...
He reached down from on high, he took me;
he drew me out of mighty waters.
He delivered me from my strong enemy,
and from those who hated me;
for they were too mighty for me...
He brought me out into a broad place;
he delivered me, because he delighted in me.
(Psalm 18:1–2, 6–8, 16–17, 19)

I picture God descending to rescue me like a mother whose fierce love, so distressed by her child's absence, can be expressed only by grabbing the child and shaking him furiously; I hear God saying to me, 'Where on earth have you been?'

Physical

This may seem a very physical picture of God reaching down to grab God's child. The Bible does tend to use physical images of the spiritual, because they are images we understand. Jesus told us that 'God is spirit' (John 4:24) but he knew we could not picture pure spirit, so we needed to think of God in terms of the physical world we live in. He talked about himself as a shepherd, a door, a vine, bread—all physical beings or objects in our world.

Novelist Joanna Trollope observed in one of her novels (sadly, I no longer remember which) that 'one of the many ways in which we love our children is how we love them physically'. There are few greater delights than holding your own infant, even when it seems to get heavier by the minute! Those unfocused eyes, those tiny fingers and even tinier fingernails, that first smile, that downy head, that clean smell of a freshly bathed baby... all these things give us immeasurable pleasure. As our children grow and learn, we continue to rejoice in their physical growth. Most homes with a child in have a growth chart on the wall, unless the parents are happy to draw lines on the door frame! This physical love is what makes us so distressed when our child acquires its first scar, as John did when he fell in that shower in Austria. (You can still see a thin line and the faint marks of stitches on his chin.)

If we have a child with a physical or learning disability, our journey in this respect may be very different. Yet even if our child is not conventionally beautiful, we love it just as much—maybe more, because of its extra needs. Does God too enjoy our physical growth? Does God feel sadness when some part of our physical being is damaged? God made us part of a physical world, after all, and that was no mistake. The early church was over-influenced by Greek ways of thinking, which valued the spiritual above the material, and traces of this influence still survive in our theology. For the Jewish writers of the Old Testament, and perhaps for the earliest Christians, too, the material *is* spiritual, because it's made by God. God must love matter, having made so much of it! There is nothing unspiritual about being physical.

I often cringe when I hear a Christian say, 'That's so human', in a context of excusing their own or someone else's sin or mistake. Human beings are frail and mistake-prone now, but we were created as the pinnacle of creation, creatures, as Psalm 8 puts it, 'a little lower than God, and crowned… with glory and honour' (v. 5). The early Church Father Irenaeus said, 'The glory of God is a human being fully alive.'[5] To call something 'human' is a compliment, not an apology. Why don't we say, 'That's so human' about a masterpiece by Michelangelo or the intricacy of a space rocket?

Perhaps God feels just as thrilled by our children's first going into adult sizes for shoes as we do; and maybe even just as saddened by our own ageing and loss of skills as we ourselves do—for the Bible tells us that ageing and death came into the world through sin: 'Therefore, just as sin came into the world through one man, and death came through sin, and so death spread to all because all have sinned' (Romans 5:12). Maybe God is just as pleased by my going to the gym and looking after the body God gave me, as by my spending an hour in prayer or reading the Bible and growing spiritually. God is, in the best sense of the word, a materialist.

A spiritual body

This has implications for our understanding of heaven and eternal destiny, too. Contrary to what Christians often say, the Bible says almost nothing about our going to heaven, or about our souls being freed from our bodies. That's that intrusive Greek thinking getting into the church again. Jewish thought regards human beings as a unity of body and spirit, and the last chapter of Revelation shows, not us being taken to heaven, but the new creation being brought to us:

Then I saw a new heaven and a new earth; for the first heaven and the first earth had passed away, and the sea was no more. And I saw the holy city, the new Jerusalem, coming down out of heaven from God, prepared as a bride adorned for her husband. And I heard a loud voice from the throne saying, 'See, the home of God is among mortals. He will dwell with them; they will be his peoples, and God himself will be with them.' (Revelation 21:1–3)

There is absolutely nothing here about our going to be with God: it's all about God's coming to be with us—which is precisely what Jesus did in his incarnation. (And why would there be an incarnation, if God so despised flesh?) Heaven, or the new creation, is very much a physical entity here, because it is made for physical beings to live in.

I have to tell a funny story here. My friend Evelyn and I were looking at a diagram in a theology book, which showed the Greek model of being human as something like this:

MIND

SPIRIT

_____

BODY

SEX

The things that were 'good' were above the line; the things that were 'bad' were below it, and only the things above the line would have any continuing life after death.

Then the book showed the Hebrew/Christian model, which looked like this:

MIND

SPIRIT

BODY

Evelyn, who is normally quite a prim and proper person, took one look and said, 'Where's the sex in the Christian one?' Where indeed? That is probably a subject for a different book.

The main point is that, in a biblical understanding, mind, body and spirit are a unity: when one dies all die, and when one is resurrected, all are resurrected. But how can we be physical beings after our bodies have rotted in the grave? Paul solves this with his concept of 'a spiritual body':

But someone will ask, 'How are the dead raised? With what kind of body do they come?' Fool! What you sow does not come to life unless it dies. And as for what you sow, you do not sow the body that is to be, but a bare seed, perhaps of wheat or of some other

grain. But God gives it a body as he has chosen, and to each kind of seed its own body… So it is with the resurrection of the dead. What is sown is perishable, what is raised is imperishable. It is sown in dishonour, it is raised in glory. It is sown in weakness, it is raised in power. It is sown a physical body, it is raised a spiritual body. If there is a physical body, there is also a spiritual body.
(1 Corinthians 15:35–38, 42–44)

All this is a mystery, as Paul himself acknowledges, but I think we can safely say that our eternal destiny is in some sense physical. Just as we love our children's 'oh-so-cuddlable' physical bodies and appearance, and we are upset when those bodies are hurt, so God loves the bodies God has given us, and is upset when something goes wrong with them. As the New Jerusalem translation puts it: 'We are God's work of art' (Ephesians 2:10). What artist, if a work of theirs is damaged, does not do all she can to restore it?

Whose child?

I think this may be the time to say something about how I am using the words 'child' and 'children' in relation to God. The Bible does not specifically state that all human beings are children of God. That would have been foreign to Hebrew thinking, for it took many centuries for the biblical writers to see that their God was the God of all creation, not just of the Jews. Nevertheless, Genesis does state that we are all in the image of God, which does inevitably suggest that God is a kind of parent and we are all his children—for what is more in the image of any human being than his or her biological children?

The New Testament does imply that, to be fully a child

of God, we have to belong to Jesus: 'But to all who received him, who believed in his name, he gave power to become children of God' (John 1:12). However, the invitation to become a child of God is to all, and God does not willingly let anyone out of God's grasp: 'The Lord is not slow about his promise, as some think of slowness, but is patient with you, not wanting any to perish, but all to come to repentance' (2 Peter 3:9).

God's deepest desire is for everyone to recognise God in Christ and to become part of the world's salvation.

I have chosen to speak of all of humanity as God's children, rather than limiting that term to people with an explicit Christian commitment. Obviously, Christians know the fatherhood/motherhood of God in a way others may not do, but I believe God wants to act as a parent to all, especially at the times when we are suffering, whether through our own fault or through circumstances beyond our control.

Chapter 5

Something wrong

Called to the head

It had been a long time since I'd been called in to see a headmistress, but the feeling of dread was still familiar and I was to become a lot more familiar with it. We'd put John in a private nursery at two and a half years of age; we thought he was ready, because he already knew his alphabet and could count. Little did I know that intellectual readiness was not the only kind. Now the nursery head had called us in because she had concerns about his behaviour: avoiding the teaching room, not playing with other children, unable to take turns, and when he did relate to other children, he was pushing and shoving them.

What does any parent think in this situation? Our first thought, since he was our only child, was that we had been too liberal and failed to discipline him properly. But as the months wore on and his 'awkwardness' did not change, we began to wonder what was going on. Soon we were attending appointments at what was then Child Guidance, where we were simply told that the two of us were not consistent in our parenting and that everything would work out if I just parented the same way as Ed (which, as he had been brought up in a very strict family and tended to copy this, I did not want to do). Then the nursery refused to take John for another year, and so he had to go back to his babyhood childminder for a couple of days a week, as I was still writing regularly.

Finally, he came up to the magical age of four, which in the UK is the ridiculously early qualifying age for 'proper school' (in spite of the fact that all the international research shows that the later children start school, the better they perform academically). I felt, as he was so young (having been born in August), that he should really be going into the nursery class, but because he had turned four two weeks before the beginning of term, the school would take him only in Reception. The school we wanted, being in the next-door borough, didn't do a mid-year intake, so he couldn't start a term or two later.

This was the start of a five-year education nightmare. John was bullied in the playground. This, I have to say, was the only thing with which the school dealt well. He was unable to sit still at circle time, or to stop touching the tempting objects around the classroom. (Why do teachers put all these objects out if they don't want the children to explore them?) By the time we were two terms in, he was hitting other children, doing all his paintings in pure black and running round the classroom tearing posters off the walls. The school's solution was to call me in whenever there was trouble, which struck me as extremely poor behaviour management: if a child isn't coping with school, and knows that making trouble is a sure-fire way to get Mum, what is he going to do?

Eventually, the school said he could attend only part-time, which was making it very hard for me to do my work, and by the end of the Easter term I had had enough. I went to fetch him on the last day of term and had to watch the teacher haranguing him for several minutes about something that had happened hours earlier, while he visibly cringed below her verbal onslaught. (To be fair to her, she was newly qualified and not coping with teaching, and I did privately pray for her. I can't say if my prayers were the reason, but after a breakdown she later became a Christian and went to work in a church school.) I decided on the spot that, since he wasn't even legally obliged to go to school yet, I was taking him out of it. Back to the childminder again…

Conditions

By this time Ed and I were beginning to read articles and books to try to identify what problem John might possibly have. We became instant experts on all kinds of conditions we had never heard of before, including 'hyperlexia', which apparently involves reading dramatically early. The only one that seemed to fit was that of 'gifted child', and we were already fairly convinced that, at least in some ways, our son was gifted. Clearly there was something else going on, but no one could tell us what it was.

I had always been a critic of traditional education, which I thought was too rigid and not child-centred enough; and I began to search for every 'alternative' school I could find—of which there are quite a few in north London. After months of searching I found a little Montessori school a short drive from our house, which was cheaper than most private schools (my mother paid, bless her), and which was willing to take John once he was five. It was based in a rather dingy and unattractive church hall, but I liked the Montessori system because it allowed the children to develop at their own pace and focussed mainly on learning in practical ways, using specially designed equipment that enabled the child to be in charge of its own learning. Not only this, but under the Montessori system, children of five are still in the informal setting of nursery: being a European system, it does not start formal classroom education until the children are six. This meant that John was in the nursery class for his first year, which we hoped would enable his emotional and social development to catch up with his academic abilities.

So began three fairly happy years for us and John. However, this school, too, had concerns about John's behaviour and his inability to relate well to other children. Also, the school did not teach children older than seven, so we knew he would have to go back to state school then or to another 'alternative' setting. The school kept saying they were going to open an older class, but it never happened, partly because they didn't really have the room, and partly because of the difficulty of recruiting Montessori teachers who are qualified to teach older children.

When he was in the Reception class of the state school, John had already been at Stage Three of the process of getting a statement of special needs (this was under the old five-stage system, which has since been changed). When his problems continued, I thought that if I contacted the local authority to ask for an educational psychologist to assess him, explaining the difficulties he was having, we would soon get a promise of help when he went back to mainstream. I was woefully ignorant of the statementing system: we were turned down at once and told that we didn't have enough evidence for him to be assessed. I waited a while and then applied again the next year, only to get the same result. In all, we applied three times in three years and were turned down every time. Even when we got a full private psychologist's report, it was not allowed as sufficient evidence. The one thing the education authority never told me was what kind of evidence they wanted!

To be fair, when confronted by a boy who has taken his seven-year-old SATS tests at six and a half and got the results typical of a nine-year-old, I can see why the LEA would wonder why there was a problem. Of course, they couldn't see him rolling on the floor in the classroom or deliberately shutting the door on other children. I think they were also unwilling to assess a child who was in private school (even though they are actually obliged to under the law), probably assuming that we could afford to keep him in private school, which we couldn't.

In the meantime, I was being diagnosed with breast cancer and had two lots of surgery and six weeks of exhausting radiotherapy, which didn't exactly make my search for the right schooling any easier.

Lopsided

The private psychologist we eventually consulted initially said that John did not have any specific condition but just 'lop-sided development'. He also said, 'It's constitutional rather than cultural.' When Ed asked what this meant, I chipped in, 'I think he means it's not our fault!'—and the psychologist agreed. Later he sent us information about a condition called Non-Verbal Learning Disorder (NLD). This consists of a large gap between verbal skills, in which John was highly developed, and so-called 'performance skills', which include things like the ability to work with 3D shapes, ability to understand someone else's motivation, ability to organise oneself, and so on. A gap of more than ten to 15 points between the two halves of the Wechsler Intelligence Scale is a cause for concern—and John had a 53-point gap! Yet even this psychologist's report didn't persuade the local authority to assess him.

Meanwhile, John left the Montessori school, and I was on a desperate hunt for more 'alternative' schooling. When I found a special needs project called 'Nature Kids', run from a teacher's home in Hertfordshire, it seemed like an ideal stopgap for a year while we continued to try to get our assessment. In the end, it turned out to be two exhausting years, during which the project moved even further away, and I was driving 16 miles each way every day to collect John. In the second year he was also a drop-in pupil at a Montessori school that took older pupils, but that was 18 miles away!

Meanwhile the 'Nature Kids' teacher, while very committed to the children and teaching virtually one-to-one, was into every alternative diet you could think of, not to mention 'natural' remedies used by those with a New Age philosophy, which she sometimes gave without asking our permission. Her main policy of taking the kids out in nature as much as possible seemed to work well, and we were happy with that. The gluten-free and dairy-free diet she prescribed was a nightmare, given that John has never consented to eat more than a couple of vegetables and that he eats absolutely no fruit, and that his favourite foods are pasta and cheese!

At last, after over three years of trying, we got an official assessment, but only because the borough's autism team leader had had a daughter in the same Montessori school, had seen John in action, and told the panel they absolutely must assess him. I am eternally grateful to her! Finally, when John had already had five years out of mainstream schooling, and only one year of primary school was left, we got our statement, with a substantial amount of support hours. We had been told we would never get more than 15 hours of support, but we got more than twice as many, and the borough agreed to send John to the school we wanted.

This school had a specialist language unit attached, where he could get help with social skills from an on-site speech therapist and could have an easier transition from a class of three to a class of 30. It was also only five minutes' walk away from our house, which was a great relief after our two years of commuting.

It was such a joy to take him less than half a mile to school, and to meet local parents with whom I could be friends. The school even had a support group for parents of children with special educational needs. Ironically, this was the school I had first wanted him to go to when he was four, but I had been put off by a local mother saying it was 'rough'. If only I'd trusted my instincts... He had a wonderful teaching assistant who, although she has now returned to her native New Zealand, recently found me through my blog (even though I don't write it in my own name) and told me she has a mug with a photo of John on it, at which she looks every day.

John mostly thrived at the school, although there were some regrettable incidents. As soon as he had settled there, we had to begin the search for a secondary school. The nightmare was not over. Later, when we had chosen a secondary school we thought was ideal (and also five minutes' walk from our house), it was soon to change its attitude to inclusion of children with special needs dramatically, with the advent of a new head master who didn't believe in inclusion. In the second year of secondary school, John was to go for a whole academic year to a residential (weekly boarding) NHS provision to help him with some problems that just weren't going away. There they re-diagnosed him as having Asperger's syndrome and possibly ADHD. He returned to his secondary school, but as I write, he has just started in a new school, having dropped out of Year 12. This is his ninth educational setting and, although he's now in a specialist resource for pupils on the autistic spectrum, I can't wait for him to leave school! (Of course, then there's college, with its own problems…)

Special children

By the time John went back into mainstream at Year 6, we were used to the idea of our child being different from others—but it was still a deep pain for both my husband and me. I had started to go to groups for parents of children on the autistic spectrum and a group that arranged holiday time activities for such children. We were learning how to be 'special parents', with all the heartache, the isolation and the fears that come along with that. Parents of 'special' children soon know that it is not only their child with whom nobody plays in the playground, but that they are the parent outside the school gates to whom none of the 'normal' parents talk. Thank God for the parents' support group at the school, even if I could never get a word in to their animated conversations!

It was around this time that I first started to reflect on my parental feelings about John, and how they might reflect God's feelings about us, God's children. Isn't there a sense in which we are all God's 'special' children? Just the other day, John announced to me out of the blue that 'human beings have been made wrong'. This led into the first 'religious' conversation I have had with him for some time. The Bible does indeed tell us that we are all 'damaged' in some way by the fallenness of the world. None of us will ever be all we could be or want to be, at least this side of the grave. We are certainly not all that God wants us to be. Every day we fail or fall, and sometimes we deliberately and rebelliously do the wrong thing. Yet God does not love us any less.

I have had many moments when I felt a huge sadness that John was different from other children, especially when I saw the pain and frustration his limitations caused him: his inability to cope with the strength of his own emotions, his difficulty in communicating what he was feeling, his isolation in social groups, his problems knowing how to relate to other children. Why, when we waited so long, did God send us a miracle baby, only for us to find out that there was 'something wrong' with him? Does God too, feel a huge sadness for the way human beings, the pinnacle of God's creation, God's representatives on earth, have gone so wrong and suffered so much?

Yes, I know, other children have far worse disabilities, and we should be grateful for what we have. I also know that some parents of children with an ASC (autistic spectrum condition), and some adults with Asperger's syndrome, say that there is nothing 'wrong' about the way people with these conditions process experience and emotions—it's just a differently wired brain, and society has to learn to accept people who have this difference. Some parents even say, 'I wouldn't have my son/daughter any other way', while autistic adults say, 'I don't need to be "cured".'

While I do understand the rationale for thinking this way, I also see the negative ways in which his difference impacts upon John, and if I could wave a magic wand and make him 'normal', I think I still would—provided he didn't become any less creative, humorous and delightful in his individuality.

I wonder whether God looks at us, his damaged, 'special' children, and wants us to stay exactly how we are. God's love for us is certainly unconditional—God loves us with all our faults, bad habits and rebelliousness. To return to Julian of Norwich's parable of the lord and the servant, I don't think the lord wants the servant to stay in the pit where he can't even turn his head and see his loving master. No, he wants to haul him out of the pit, heal his wounds and distress, and relate to him as a dear servant and friend. God surely wants to correct our faults, make us kingdom people and change us into the image of Jesus: 'For those whom he foreknew he also predestined to be conformed to the image of his Son, in order that he might be the firstborn within a large family' (Romans 8:29).

Flaws into features

Actually, I think it's a little more complex than that. Children with autism often have outstanding abilities and interests in one particular field, although only 10 per cent have an extreme, 'autistic savant' ability like the character in the film *Rain Man* (Dir. Barry Levinson, 1988). Their visual memory, attention to detail and at times intense concentration can give them a head start in certain jobs, if their other needs are met. So there is a sense in which what is seen as a flaw—for instance, the extreme difficulty of getting John's attention when he is 'in his own world'—can also be a strength: when he is engaged by something, he can be very determined in carrying it out.

As we 'walk in the Spirit', I suspect that God is not in the business of erasing or wiping out our failings. Being in the redemption or reclamation business, God transforms our weaknesses into strengths, and the things we or others find irritating into gifts we can share. Just as the resurrected body of Jesus still showed the scars of his crucifixion but translated from marks of shame into emblems of glory, so we, when we are transformed into all God wants us to be, may perhaps still bear the scars of our weaknesses, of the bad things that have happened to us, and the mistakes we have made—but they will be transformed into badges of victory.

When John achieves something I never expected, my joy in his development is made keener by knowing that whatever he achieves has cost him much more labour and thought than it might cost the average child. The other day he went out with his newly acquired debit card (at 16 he acquired a bank account, so that he could receive his own Disability Living Allowance) and came back after he had bought a whole new outfit, including a leather jacket and a very stylish hat. This was the first time he had been clothes shopping on his own. Other children may have reached this stage earlier, but I bet their parents weren't as pleased and proud of them as I was of John.

If we are God's 'special children', each with our own challenges that hold us back from being Christ-like, will God not be inordinately proud when, with the help of God's Spirit, we do something good that we've never done before—say, forgiving someone or performing an exceptionally generous act?

Adopted?

As well as sadness, children with disabilities can call out a great deal of love from those around them, even sometimes from people who just meet them in the street. Sadly, some parents will reject a seriously disabled child at birth, or later, when the parent just can't cope. This is where adoptive parents can and transform a child's life. Because of the legalisation of abortion, with the result that fewer unwanted babies are being born, most children available for adoption these days have a disability, or are older and very traumatised, or need to be kept with their siblings. This makes adoption a considerably harder option than it used to be. It is one of the reasons why Ed and I, when we were struggling with infertility, were very ambivalent about the idea of adopting, especially as I had no experience with small children. Yet amazingly, infertile couples, or couples who already have children, or even single people who still want a child, come forward to take on some of these children with all their difficulties. If only there were more of these brave people around!

I have talked so far in terms of us all being God's children, whether we know it or not. A lot of talk about God's 'parent-hood' in the Bible is actually framed in terms of adoption. Paul uses this image repeatedly to describe our relationship with God as Christians:

But when the fullness of time had come, God sent his Son, born of a woman, born under the law, in order to redeem those who were under the law, so that we might receive adoption as children. (Galatians 4:4–5)

For you did not receive a spirit of slavery to fall back into fear, but you have received a spirit of adoption. When we cry, 'Abba! Father!' it is that very Spirit bearing witness with our spirit that we are children of God, and if children, then heirs, heirs of God and joint heirs with Christ—if, in fact, we suffer with him so that we may also be glorified with him. (Romans 8:15–17)

Later, Paul talks of our final redemption, the putting of all things right, as our adoption:

We know that the whole creation has been groaning in labour pains until now; and not only the creation, but we ourselves, who have the first fruits of the Spirit, groan inwardly while we wait for adoption, the redemption of our bodies. (vv. 22–23)

It is as though, by humanity's falling away from God, we have ceased to be automatically God's children. Now, to experience God as our parent again, we have to be adopted back into God's family. Yet our final adoption, the redemption of our physical selves and our world, is still to come.

The novel *A Simple Life* by Rosie Thomas (Arrow Books, 2003), tells the story of a woman whose first child was born with Down's syndrome, and who gave her up for adoption at birth. Later, when her child is a teenager, she fears she has done the wrong thing and goes in search of her child, even kidnapping her for a while from her adoptive parents. At last, however, she realises that her daughter's 'true' parents are those who have cared for and loved her since her babyhood, and who love her just as much as they would love a 'normal' child. Biology is not everything.

My mother's story is similarly instructive. She was the child of a Jewish refugee who fled from Poland to Vienna and had been separated from her husband on her journey from Poland. She was pregnant on her journey and gave birth to my mother in Vienna and then put all the children into an orphanage or foster care, as she had no means to support them. (She died a few years later in the 'Spanish flu' epidemic that killed so many after World War I. Having a biological grandmother who died in 1919 makes me feel ancient!)

My mother was eventually fostered by a childless Jewish couple; the law didn't allow them to adopt until the husband was 50. During her first couple of years with them, her birth father turned up and wanted to see her. An appointment was made at the appropriately named 'Hotel Kummer'—*Kummer* is a German word for care or worry. Her prospective adoptive parents were terrified that the birth father might take her away. As it happened, her father never turned up, so they were able to go on to adopt her. (He too died young, in 1926, so it is probably a good thing he hadn't taken her back.)

I have the name and birth and death dates of my biological grandmother and sometimes think about trying to trace her family. My mother's older brother turned up in 1927, when he was 18 and she was 12, to tell her that he was trying to emigrate to Israel. If he made it there, I could have a whole tribe of first cousins in Israel. My mother has no interest at all in tracing her birth family: to her, her adoptive parents were her 'real parents', even for the relatively short time she had them. (Her adoptive father died of lung cancer when my mother was 16, and her adoptive mother perished in the Holocaust when my mother was in her mid-20s.)

I find in these two stories, one fictional and one real, a good picture of our 'adoption' by God. It is the parent who cares for the child, not the parent with a 'blood tie', who is the 'real' mother or father. You could say that we do have a 'blood tie' with God, for it is the shedding of Jesus' blood that has opened our way to a parent–child relationship with God:

Therefore, my friends, since we have confidence to enter the sanctuary by the blood of Jesus, by the new and living way that he opened for us through the curtain (that is, through his flesh), and since we have a great priest over the house of God, let us approach with a true heart in full assurance of faith. (Hebrews 10:19–22)

I find the cross of Christ a great mystery. I certainly don't know how it 'works', and there are several different ways of explaining it. Viewing it as a substitutionary sacrifice depends very much on the sacrificial system that first-century Jews had, and it can be hard for modern people, who do not have that system, to understand the cross that way. I do know that somehow through his life, death and resurrection, Jesus conquered evil and broke down the dividing wall that our fallenness had put between us and God. He also broke down the wall that existed between Jews and Gentiles at the time:

But now in Christ Jesus you who once were far off have been brought near by the blood of Christ. For he is our peace; in his flesh he has made both groups into one and has broken down the dividing wall, that is, the hostility between us. He has abolished the law with its commandments and ordinances, that he might create in himself one new humanity in place of the two, thus making peace. (Ephesians 2:13–15)

If the Jewish people thought of themselves as being automatically God's children, or at least as the children of Abraham, then here they are being told that both they and the Gentiles needed to be adopted into Christ—which must have been quite offensive to the Jews.

Chosen

I wasn't told about my mother's adoption until I was already an adult. It was a shock to me, at over the age of 30, to discover that the grandmother who had died in the Holocaust long before my birth, and who I had heard so much about, was not in fact my biological grandmother.

It felt as though my mother had become a totally different person. (Apparently, she had planned to tell me when I got married—obviously by the time I hit 30 she had given up on my ever getting married!) I found it strange that she had a feeling of shame and embarrassment about having been adopted, even though her birth parents had been married and there was nothing 'suspect' about her origins. Overall, however, she counts herself as having been extremely lucky to survive and have good adoptive parents whom she loved and who brought her up well.

By now I am completely used to her story, and it helps me to think about what it means to be adopted into God's family. The difference between a 'natural' child and an adopted one is that an adopted child is consciously chosen, and adoptive parents often highlight this to encourage their children when the children feel 'different'. Perhaps thinking of ourselves as adopted children of God can help us feel accepted by God— for we didn't 'just happen' to our divine father, but he chose each of us deliberately. Jesus says to his disciples, 'You did not choose me but I chose you. And I appointed you to go and bear fruit, fruit that will last, so that the Father will give you whatever you ask him in my name' (John 15:16).

Perhaps this biblical image of adoption can help adoptive parents realise that they are not 'second-class parents' but special people who have been given the privilege, of choosing the unwanted or the damaged, with the task of restoring them to belonging and wholeness, just as God does. To adopt a child, especially a child with a disability, is to reflect God's love in a very special way. Birth parents who have a child with special needs have to cope with it, because this is what they have been given—they are often heroic, but adoptive parents who take on this task are even greater heroes.

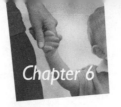

Chapter 6

Discipline

Aliens

A Mennonite parenting book I read some years ago[1] includes a chapter telling the story of a couple who encounter two little aliens. The aliens are very lovable, about three feet tall, with big eyes, soft faces, sweet smiles and strokeable, shining hair. The couple decide to adopt them into their family.

All is not well, however. As time goes on, it becomes clear that the aliens have no idea how to behave on earth. It all comes to a head when one of the aliens throws a tantrum in a hardware store, because its parents won't buy it a chainsaw for Christmas.

'Chainsaw for Christmas' has become a saying in our house for any situation in which our son wants something that would not actually be good for him. The book that tells the story of the little aliens also describes children as 'apprentice human beings', another phrase that has entered our family language. Apprentices need to be taught, not just the skills of their trade, but also how to behave as whatever they are apprenticed to become. They need the guidance of an older, wiser, more trained and experienced master (or mistress). My husband has taken on several casual assistants in his plumbing and gas fitting business, sometimes from among clients from our local soup kitchen, or people who were recovering from mental health problems. It has become quite clear that an 'apprenticeship' is as much hard work for the master as it is for the pupil. Guiding someone into 'the ways of work' is a demanding task, and it's fair to say that having an assistant has sometimes made his life harder rather than easier.

Mistakes

If children are 'apprentice human beings', then the task of parents is to introduce them to the rules of human life: how to relate to others, how to work, and ideally how to relate to God.

When John was small, I was not very keen on the whole idea of discipline. My own upbringing had been, as I saw it, very liberal, and yet I had turned out reasonably well (well, perhaps you should ask my friends and family whether that is true). I tried to encourage John in his exploration of the world and to restrict him as little as possible. Ed, on the other hand, had what he describes as 'a Victorian upbringing', with clear rules—children obeyed parents, and parents were not averse to using the slipper for punishment. He didn't want to reproduce this in our life with John and at first went along with my way of doing things. It soon became clear, with the help of Child Guidance and other sources of advice, that Ed knew something I didn't: that children need clear boundaries to feel safe and to help them learn. It took some years for us to learn how to 'sing off the same hymn sheet' as far as disciplining John went, and as he grows up and changes, we are still on that learning curve.

Learners inevitably make mistakes, and I bitterly regret some of the ones I made, especially the small number of times I smacked John (which, as a pacifist, I felt very ambivalent about) and the extreme measures I took like once locking him in his bedroom for a short while. I can only say that bringing up a child on the autistic spectrum is measurably harder than bringing up a 'neurotypical' child. With my shortage of family, and Ed's family being a couple of hundred miles away, we did not always have the support we might have needed. (My parents, aged 78 and 80 when John was born, still took him out in the buggy, walking a mile to a local café, every Saturday morning to give us a break, for three years.) Also, not every babysitter has the skills to cope with a child with an ASC (autistic spectrum condition), so it was not always easy to take a break. We have, however, always had fantastic support from our Mennonite church; and for six months when John was a baby we had a lovely neighbour who came in every day to hold him for three hours while I had a sleep and caught up on household admin. He would always go straight to sleep in her arms, whereas in mine he'd perversely stay awake!

From early on, we had input from state agencies such as Child Guidance, which later became Child and Adolescent Mental Health Services. This 'help' was not always welcome, at least on my part, because it required me to change my way of parenting, and change is always difficult. The big differences between Ed's upbringing and mine were a constant obstacle. I did come to realise that there were also rules in my own upbringing; it was just that they were unspoken (and unspoken rules are the very thing that a child on the autistic spectrum like John has difficulty perceiving or understanding).

As John grew and changed, so our approach to setting boundaries had, and still has, to develop with him. There are always new issues to deal with, especially as he grows into an adult who can make his own choices. For a childless woman,

Julian of Norwich has great insight into the way parents adapt to their children's growth:

The kind, loving mother who knows and sees the need of her child guards it very tenderly, as the nature and condition of motherhood will have. And always as the child grows in age and in stature, she acts differently, but she does not change her love. And when it is even older, she allows it to be chastised to destroy its faults, so as to make the child receive virtues and grace.[2]

On the street not long ago I overheard a mother with two small daughters say to one of them, 'If I said "Yes" to everything you asked for, would that make me a good mother?' The little girl was old enough to understand what she was saying, and agreed that no, it would not make her a good mother. Another case of 'chainsaw for Christmas'!

If God gave us everything we asked for, would that be a sign of a good God? Not necessarily: we might ask for things that would be very bad for us. Certainly, if God had given me everything I asked for in the past, I would have been married much earlier, but probably to entirely the wrong person. Farmers who need rain are not best pleased when someone else prays for sunny weather!

Here's how the writer of Hebrews (a favourite Bible book of mine) puts it:

And you have forgotten the exhortation that addresses you as children—

'My child, do not regard lightly the discipline of the Lord, or lose heart when you are punished by him; for the Lord disciplines those whom he loves, and chastises every child whom he accepts.'

Endure trials for the sake of discipline. God is treating you as children; for what child is there whom a parent does not discipline? If you do not have that discipline in which all children share, then you are illegitimate and not his children. Moreover, we had human parents to discipline us, and we respected them. Should we not be even more willing to be subject to the father of spirits and live? For they disciplined us for a short time as seemed best to them, but he disciplines us for our good, in order that we may share his holiness. Now, discipline always seems painful rather than pleasant at the time, but later it yields the peaceful fruit of righteousness to those who have been trained by it. (Hebrews 12:5–11)

God's discipline, the writer tells us, is a sign of God's love. I have to say that there are days when I find myself thinking that God must love me more than others, since God seems to allow me to go through more trials and hardships than some other people I know! God must love our little church a lot, too, judging by the amount of 'chastisement' it has received in recent years… It is reassuring to read in Hebrews that 'discipline' or difficulties in our lives are the mark of a true disciple or a true church.

I don't believe the Bible is saying here that God deliberately sends difficult times our way so as to make us grow. That would not be the action of a loving parent. In fact, the writer was writing to believers who were facing persecution, and he would be unlikely to suggest that God had initiated the persecution! I believe it means that we are given freedom to choose our own actions. In the story of Adam and Eve, the first humans are given a free choice: they may eat fruit from all the trees but one—and of course, with regard to that one, they make the wrong choice. Yet God does not give up on them but continues to protect them as they leave the innocent state of Eden.

In our freedom, we will encounter difficulties and trials, but God uses these hard times to help us mature in Christ. This fits in well with modern understandings of parental discipline: within the bounds of safety, the parent should allow the child to experience the negative consequences of bad behaviour, rather than imposing an arbitrary punishment. This is perhaps even more important with children 'on the spectrum', who often find it hard to understand for what they are being punished, since the punishment may bear no obvious relation to what they have done or failed to do.

Not only punishment

The Bible does use the words 'punished' and 'chastises' in Hebrews 12 (at least the NRSV translation does—others have 'rebukes' or 'corrects', which perhaps have a less negative ring). I don't think this means that discipline is only about punishment. One thread that has run through all the various parenting courses and advice we have had is that it is more important to reward positive behaviour than to punish negative behaviour. It always struck me as rather ironic that the authorities would constantly stress this approach, and yet they never seemed to use the approach themselves with the parents! We were desperate to do well, yet in almost every case it seemed to be us, the parents, who were in the wrong. There was one notable exception, when John went into the NHS unit previously mentioned for an academic year. The teachers and therapists there were unfailingly affirming to the parents whose children had been admitted—perhaps that's why they were voted the best psychiatric team in the country!

Does God, too, take the approach of affirming the behaviour God wants from us, rather than punishing our sins? Jesus' behaviour towards people in need suggests that this is indeed what God does. It is true that Jesus sometimes tongue-lashed people and called them rude names such a 'brood of vipers' (Matthew 12:34). But he did this only when he was speaking to the scribes and Pharisees, who thought themselves already morally better than the mass of humanity. Affirming their behaviour would just have confirmed them in their view of their own righteousness. When he speaks to the ordinary people, he is gentle and affirmative. What could be more affirming to the disciples than to be told, 'You are the light of the world' (5:14)? (Note that etymological link between 'disciples' and 'discipline'—a disciple is one learning a discipline.) I heard Radio 2 presenter Jeremy Vine (who himself is a Christian) declare: 'You can't make people nicer by punishing them,' and I think he's right. Even God has chosen to take our punishment himself on the cross, rather than imposing it on us. God's 'discipline' is gentle, tender and adapted to the individual.

I want to add a rider here. Some Christians are fond of quoting, 'God is faithful, and he will not let you be tested beyond your strength' (1 Corinthians 10:13). Yet it seems patently obvious that some people are tested beyond their strength. Even Christians may commit suicide, or do something else drastic, like leaving a spouse. How do we understand this?

I think there are a couple of ways of approaching this. First, Paul is addressing a community here rather than an individual; the 'you' is plural. He is not actually saying that no individual will be tested beyond their strength; he is saying that the community will not be tested beyond its communal strength. There is strength in a community which is greater than the sum of the individuals who make it up because the Holy Spirit is given to the community of Christians.

Secondly, we are not expected to rely just on our own strength to get us through crises. We are meant to access the strength of God. A person who is feeling suicidal may not be able to believe in that strength in the time of their crisis. It is impossible for a person to be tested *beyond God's strength*, but it is possible for them to be tested *beyond the strength they believe themselves to have*. When it seems we are tested beyond what we can bear, it may be that we are being tested only beyond what we believe ourselves able to bear. The strength of God, if only we can believe in it, is infinite. After all, God in Christ endured death and came back from it.

I have made this detour because I think it is not the whole picture to say that God's discipline is always tender and compassionate. It may well not seem so to us at the time. Hebrews acknowledges that 'discipline always seems painful rather than pleasant at the time' (12:11). The key word is 'seems'.

When I have had to prevent John from doing something, or to rebuke him for something that he had done, it no doubt seemed to him that I was the worst mother in the world and was making his life a misery. In the midst of a tantrum, he literally could not see that I was expressing my deep love for him by restricting him or correcting him—just as the servant in Julian of Norwich's parable of the lord and the servant could not turn his head to see his master continuing to look at him 'with pity, not with blame'.

I've often heard exasperated parents exclaim, 'I'm going to kill you if you do X again!' Of course for the vast majority of parents this is a completely empty threat, and one I have taken care never to use. No loving parent would ever actually carry out that threat, but even the good parent may sometimes feel like killing their child, when the child is annoying beyond endurance. Yet a child who is genuinely loved knows deep down that its parent/s will never deliberately do it harm. Do we as children of God have that same confidence in God's good will towards us?

Letting us learn

I do not want to suggest here that God will miraculously rescue us from every bad situation in which we find ourselves. That would not necessarily be a sign of love. We may need to stay in difficult situations in order to learn things—emotionally, intellectually and spiritually (and even physically)—that we need to learn. A good parent does not always intervene to help a child who is learning, for example, how to tie shoelaces or how to get on with other children. If we intervene too much, being what is now called a 'helicopter parent' (always hovering around), we will stall the process of our children learning for themselves.

You may have already heard a version of the story I am about to tell. A child was watching a butterfly struggling to wriggle free of its cocoon. The child, distressed by the difficulty the butterfly was having, took a pair of scissors and cut open the cocoon to help it. The butterfly emerged, but it was weak and unable to fly and soon died. It needed the process of getting out of the cocoon to strengthen its wing muscles and turn it into the flyer it was meant to be.

If I have any criticism of my own parents (and I loved them very much and think they were good parents), it is not so much that they tried to cut open the cocoon for me and my brother, but that to some extent they tried to keep us in a cocoon for ever. My mother's anxiety, born of her difficult life experience, often kept us more protected and sheltered than was perhaps good for us. This changed a lot for me when I became a teenager, since by then my parents were very preoccupied with my brother's mental health problems, and I was left to my own devices quite a bit. Given some of the situations I got into, especially in my later teens, I am quite surprised I was never raped or murdered! But my parents had instilled enough good sense in me to avoid the worst things in which I could have got involved. Besides, I became a Christian at 16 (my parents were at my baptism and were visibly moved), so I had some pretty clear boundaries for myself. My 'testimony' is very boring since I didn't have enough time as a non-Christian to indulge in any spectacular and 'exciting' sins. In fact, I was a distressingly moralistic teenager—I hope that the longer I am a Christian, the less judgmental I get.

For God to shelter us from every risk, like an over-protective parent, would not necessarily be a good way of acting towards us. Think of Psalm 23, so often used as a comfort to those going through trouble. 'The Lord is my shepherd…' (v. 1)—but notice that the psalm does not portray God as miraculously 'airlifting' the psalmist from the 'valley of the shadow of death', or showing him an alternative route. No, it merely tells us that the psalmist will fear no evil, because God is with him: 'Even though I walk through the darkest valley, I fear no evil; for you are with me; your rod and your staff—they comfort me' (Psalm 23:4).

The original meaning of the English word 'comfort' was to strengthen or to urge onward—you could 'comfort' someone with a sharp poke with a cattle prod! We will all, at some point, have dark valleys in our life, and we have to go through, not around them. The valley may be too dark for the traveller to 'see' God, but it does not mean God is not there.

Birds in their nests agree?

There is one aspect of parental discipline of which I have no experience, because I have only one child: sibling rivalry. I have indeed had a sibling, but because my brother was over five years older than me and we were different sexes, there was never any real conflict between us. He was always very fond of me and affectionate towards me, apparently ever since I was born.

John has had a 'church brother' in the shape of his best friend from church, who frequently used to stay with us and at whose house John frequently stayed. Not being real brothers, they were in no competition for parental attention, and I can only ever recall them having a real row once—a row which deeply upset both of them because they really liked each other and thought they had destroyed their friendship (they hadn't, of course). John does have one younger friend, a boy with Asperger's syndrome like himself, with whom he can get into conflict at times, but I am actually quite impressed with how patient he can be with this 'virtual younger brother'. He might not be so patient if he actually had to live with this boy all the time!

In the much-loved (at least by girls) children's novel *Little Women* by Louisa May Alcott (first published 1868), there is a scene in which Beth, the 'good' sister, remarks on her sisters' conflict by saying ironically, 'Birds in their little nests agree', a phrase that has stuck with me. I'm not sure baby birds do actually agree—after all, they are constantly in competition for the food the mother or father bird brings back. What I can say with confidence is that siblings rarely do agree, especially if they are close in age. As apprentice human beings, they are learning to share, to communicate and to care for each other and, being only learners, along the way they are bound to get it wrong a lot of the time. It seems keeping the offspring from each others' throats is a large part of the parenting task for any parent with more than one child. Siblings will inevitably compete for the best toys, for parental attention, for space in the house and space in the family. This is a vital part of their learning to negotiate with other people.

Being a sibling of a child with a special need is particularly difficult, because your sibling may be getting a lot more parental input than you are; and often you are not allowed to be anything other than patient or loving to your sibling because of its particular needs. You may even find yourself in the position of carer for your sibling at times, and this role can increase as parents get older, and especially when they die and the 'normal' siblings are left to care for the one with additional needs. I think I can get a small glimpse of how this must feel from my own experience of having a brother with mental health problems, but it must be even harder if, perhaps from your birth, you have always seen your sibling getting more time and attention. Nowadays there are groups that exist to support the siblings of children with special needs or mental health problems, which weren't around when I was going through my brother's illness.

Sisters in the Lord

Parents can get very upset when their children, all of whom they love, get into conflict. Our rose-tinted idea of a happy family can be severely tested by sibling rivalries. Is it perhaps the same for God, as God sees the human race, including Christians, full of conflict and ready to destroy each other's livelihoods or even lives? Does God grieve at God's children being so little able to get on with each other?

I once preached a sermon on Philippians 4:2–3, about a couple of women who were clearly having what would now be called 'issues' with each other: 'I urge Euodia and I urge Syntyche to be of the same mind in the Lord. Yes, and I ask you also, my loyal companion, help these women, for they have struggled beside me in the work of the gospel.'

In my sermon I imagined these two Christian leaders (for the context suggests this is what they were) as two intelligent, perhaps well educated, strong-minded women who each had fervently held opinions as to how things should be done in the church. I pointed out that such women, even in today's church, find it hard to get their gifts and callings recognised by the church, and that some churches will appoint one token woman to a senior place, but not two. I pictured two highly talented women, each of whom wanted very much to hold on to the privileges and responsibilities they had worked so hard to acquire. Even today it is sometimes hard for a woman who has found her way to the 'top' to allow other women to share that place with her. I do have to admit that I had in mind two particular women in our church at that time!

We see from the story of Euodia and Syntyche, as from the story of Paul's conflict with Barnabas (Acts 15:36–40), that the early church was no more immune to disagreement and conflict than ours is today. My church's study centre, the London Mennonite Centre, was involved in setting up a mediation and conflict resolution service called Bridge-Builders, which was originally meant to be a neighbourhood mediation service. It rapidly became clear that the amount of conflict in the neighbourhood was much more than its small staff could handle, and since then it has specialised in training Christian leaders in mediation, and going in to churches who are in danger of splitting, to try to resolve their conflict in a way that leaves everyone happy. There is absolutely no shortage of requests for their services! Of course there has always been conflict in the Christian church—the crusaders, for instance, killed hundreds or maybe thousands of fellow Christians, as well as their fellow human beings of Jewish or Muslim faith.

At the London Mennonite Centre there is a poster that puts forward a 'modest proposal': 'Let the Christians of the world agree that they will not kill each other.' On reflection, it is actually a very radical proposal, since a soldier, especially in modern warfare, cannot possibly know which of the victims of the bomb he drops are Christians. If implemented, it would mean Christians had to refuse to go to war at all—and what impact that might have on our world!

I wonder if God looks at the world, and at the churches, with deep distress at the hatred, the prejudice, the exclusion and even the killing that persists through the centuries. I wonder if God longs for God's children, whether or not they know they are God's children, to recognise that they are brothers and sisters who have to share a planet with ultimately limited resources, and that, if they can't get on, they are going to end up destroying not only each other, but the planet.

No shortage

A good parent has enough love to go round all of his or her children, but inevitably one child will always feel left out or unfairly singled out for criticism. A parent's strength and understanding are limited: we cannot do a perfect job even for one child, let alone several. I have absolutely no idea how parents of six or seven or even nine children manage! It must be—and friends with large families have confirmed this—that the older children get landed with much of the task of bringing up the younger. This can be both something that helps them mature and (perhaps at the same time) a duty they may actually resent.

It is not so with God. There is enough of God's love and power to go round seven billion humans and even more. In theory, then, we should not have to be in conflict about the world's resources, let alone about issues of faith. We persist in acting, however, as if we can have enough only at the expense of others. I think this must make God, who made this world with an ever-renewing abundance of what we need to live, very unhappy.

We are on a finite planet, and resources such as fossil fuels will run out or may be too costly to the environment. It may also be true that the planet cannot support many more people than it currently has. It is also true that with a fairer world economy, and with the political will to share the earth's resources out more justly, we might be entirely surprised at how well we could all manage. We do not have enough for everyone to live at the level of the wealthiest (which, on a world level, includes anyone likely to read this book). However, we very likely have enough for everyone to have adequate food, shelter, work and education, if only the planet's resources were distributed better. Population growth falls with greater prosperity, so the best thing we could do to limit the world's population would be to address the extreme poverty in which a huge proportion of the world's population still lives. Could global justice, in which all the people of the earth recognise that they are brothers and sisters of the same family, be a higher priority for God than whether we have our doctrines right or have the 'right' views on personal morality?

I think that as a perfect parent, God must be very concerned not only with how we act individually, but with how we get on with each other. Our human quarrels, whether within or outside the body of those who consciously identify as themselves as Christians, must be a source of great disappointment to the God who longs to parent us all. How much we could please God by resolving them!

Chapter 7

Teenage traumas

'The worst kind'

'I think I'm turning into the worst kind of teenager,' remarked John one day when he was about eleven. I didn't enquire further as to what made him think this or what 'the worst kind of teenager' did—I figured that I would find out soon enough! Indeed it didn't take many years until we reached the phase when, if he even heard our footsteps walking past the door of his bedroom (or should I say 'lair'?), he would exclaim in a grumpy voice, 'What?' It seemed parents existed purely for two purposes: asking him to do things he didn't want to and embarrassing him in public. Actually, he's still in that phase, so perhaps I'd better not let him read this bit!

My mother, who was born in 1915, is fond of saying that teenagers hadn't been invented in her day. Speaking from the point of view of advertising to the youth market, that's true. I was born at the tail end of the post-war baby boom and am therefore one of the first or perhaps second generation to be known as teenagers. Nevertheless, I do know that my mother had endless rows with her mother when my mother was in her teens, usually about boyfriends or about coming home late. There comes a time in every child's life when it is taking the first tentative steps at growing up, and there seems to be no other way to do this than to begin to rebel against one's parents, at least in one's views, if not in one's actions.

I was a rather weird teenager in that my main attempt

at rebellion against my parents consisted of becoming a Christian, something that didn't bother them at all and that had the effect, if anything, of making me more moral, or at least moralistic (I was a very priggish and judgmental girl). I watched (and disapproved!) as friends around me got into sex, drugs and rock and roll—it was the 1960s, after all. I managed to get into rock and roll but my Christian faith stopped me trying the other two. I have to admit that I sometimes wish I had gone off the rails more—at least it would give me a more sensational testimony!

Stages

The American sociologist James Fowler identified six 'stages of faith', from childhood to middle age,[1] which show how our faith develops and changes as we grow in experience and understanding. The psychiatrist M. Scott Peck amalgamated them into four stages,[2] which cover roughly the same ground. Stage 1 is the stage of chaotic desires and egocentrism, in which the individual basically does what they want and believes the world revolves around them. (This is not necessarily a bad thing: small babies need to focus primarily on what they need to stay alive.) The second stage is the stage of conformity, during which the individual learns (or perhaps creates) a set of rules and has a black-and-white understanding of good and evil. This could coincide with being at primary school, where such an attitude can be very useful. Stage 3 is the 'adolescent' stage, when the child begins to question and rebel against what it has been taught and tries to discover its own values. The last stage is that of integration, when the mature person brings together their earlier beliefs and their questioning, and emerges with a thought-through faith, a 'grown-up' faith, if you like.

The stages are not simply a progression from less good to better. Each one is necessary and serves particular purposes in our development. Nor are they necessarily linked to the phases of physically growing up. In fact, people are more likely to cycle around them at various times in their lives. A middle-aged person may be stuck in stage 2, wanting everything clear-cut and indisputable. They may even be still in stage 1, or revert to this stage, focusing mainly on their own desires. (Could this be the explanation for many a male mid-life crisis, expressed in buying a motorbike and getting a younger wife?)

It is tempting to label particular expressions of faith as belonging to particular stages of this faith journey. A very strict and separatist sect, for example, may be an example of stage 2 faith. We should remember, though, that we are meant to judge our own progress in spirituality, not someone else's—better to root out immature responses in ourselves.

As I come to talk about my son's teenage years, I can see the parallels with stage 3, when the believer starts to question the beliefs and way of life they have been taught in the past. This may be a particularly difficult time for those who have been brought up in the Christian faith, especially if it is in a very rule-based form of it. It is often the point at which people change or leave church, some never to come back. Others may label them as backsliders, or say judgmentally, 'S/he was never a real Christian anyway.' This would be a mistake! Stage 3 is a necessary stage in coming to a mature faith, a faith that is owned by the person and not just handed down by others. If we too hastily reject the questions of those who find themselves at stage 3, they may never get any further but just conclude that Christian faith is not for them.

Is it really all right to question everything you have hitherto believed? Or to question God's goodness or even existence? Many feel that by rebelling against the faith in which they have been brought up, or the faith of their youth, they are rejecting God altogether. If their questions don't come to any resolution, they may conclude that they are better off without God, and their faith will be in ruins.

As I have pointed out, though, it is perfectly normal for a teenager to struggle against their parents' wishes and values. Indeed, it is necessary in order for them to form an individual personality and set of values. The good parent recognises this and rides the storm, trusting that the attitudes they have tried to instil from their child's early childhood will somehow persist and inform their child's views as it grows up.

Parenting an adolescent is in some ways just like parenting a toddler—you get the same tantrums, and you have to hold your breath the same way as your child takes its first wobbly steps unaided. Letting go is difficult, but it has to be done. There are amazing rewards too, as our children increasingly surprise us with their independent thoughts and actions. I would far rather hear John express an opinion that he has thought through himself, even if I disagree with it, than hear him simply parrot views he has heard from us, which any fool can do.

Is God really any different? Maybe God looks at our little rebellions and faith crises and thinks, 'It's all right. I know she's going to grow out of it.' God may even be pleased that the person has started to investigate the truth of their faith for themselves, rather than taking it second-hand from others. If our Christian faith is grounded in a good image of God (rather than an image of God as an angry, easily offended ruler whose chief activity is disapproving of things), then as we grow and question, surely the best of what we have learned about God's love will persist and still be there as we rethink and reintegrate our faith.

The book of Job is a great place for discovering that questions about God do not actually destroy God. God is not an insecure father who can cope only by imposing unbendable rules on his children and dominating their every moment and thought. Paul did say to the Corinthians, 'We destroy arguments and every proud obstacle raised up against the knowledge of God, and we take every thought captive to obey Christ' (2 Corinthians 10:4–5). I do not think he meant that 'we dare not think anything that might be construed as questioning our faith'. Clearly, Paul's objective was that people should have 'the knowledge of God' and should 'obey Christ'. Our questions often bring us to a greater knowledge of God and a more informed and wholehearted obedience to Christ. Job, at the end of the Bible book, is praised for having spoken rightly about God, with all his questions—while his friends, who had any number of pat answers, are told they have spoken wrongly.

Its ugly head

The teenage years are also, of course, the time when sex rears its ugly head—although why something so potentially beautiful should be regarded as ugly, I have no idea. I noticed that my son was interested in girls from an early age, and girls showed an interest in him too—his first 'date' was when he was six. (Don't worry, they met in the playground with mothers in attendance.) Both of his two past girlfriends asked him out. I'm not sure he would know how to ask a girl! (Sadly, they both dumped him as well—could be something to do with the fact that every time the first one rang up, he would always say, 'I'm busy.') He went out with the first girlfriend when he was only 13 and she was 14, but I still got a bit worried when I found out that when he went for a sleepover at her house, her parents put them in the same room. I immediately asked them not to do this again. They were thinking of him and her either as much younger than they in fact were, or as much older!

Children learn about sex, as they have always done, in the playground, but they also learn about it at school at ever younger ages. I don't mind my son's knowing the basic facts, but I do hope that he is also being taught that sex is not a casual recreation but belongs in a committed adult relationship—preferably within marriage. This is what we have taught him at home, but I sometimes fear that he is learning something very different among his fellow pupils. However, one of the advantages of Asperger's syndrome is that it makes him less responsive to peer pressure.

We Christians don't have a very good record when it comes to dealing with sex. For centuries we have talked as though illicit sex was the biggest sin you could possibly commit, and as though God grudgingly accepts marital sex but really doesn't want to have anything to do with it. Things are changing, but we are still not very good at remembering that God made sex and wants us to enjoy it.

As a parent I still cling to the wish that my son would reserve sex for marriage, but I also recognise that, sadly, this is increasingly unlikely. And I don't really have the right to object to him indulging in 'heavy petting', since I did the same in my single years! What I can do is to make my views clear to him and to encourage him to learn how to communicate with girls so he can learn what a good relationship really is.

I wonder if God, as our parent, takes a similar attitude. It may be that God isn't half as shocked by sexual sins as we church people are. I'm not saying that God condones them but that God is just as concerned that we live just lives and minister to the poor as about whether a relationship has legal status or not. We have had a long debate in our church about whether a couple who have lived together for over 20 years are entitled to join us as members without getting married. There are strong arguments on both sides, but I do wonder whether God is simply pleased that they are committed to each other and have stayed together for so long. Which is more moral: a faithful unmarried couple, or a marriage characterised by violence or unfaithfulness?

I would like my son to get married and to be happy and faithful in his marriage. That is still my ideal. If, when he grows up, he has a girlfriend to whom he is seriously committed for the long term, and he lives with her rather than getting married, I will do everything I can to help them make their relationship last. I believe God would help me and them. Most parents mainly want their children to be happy, and I'm not sure God is any different.

True, God does not want people to be happy in a state of rebellion against God. It may sound shocking, but I sometimes wonder whether God might not prefer us to be happy sinners rather than miserable believers! A parent wants their child to have moral values but they also want their child to be fulfilled, to have friends, to be content with their life. If we think that all God is interested in is that we do the right thing, then we may be very moral but deeply resentful of the demands God makes on us—and this is not a great way to follow Jesus. Remember, 'God loves a *cheerful* giver' (2 Corinthians 9:7, emphasis mine).

Unhappy

There comes a time for every parent, however, when they are seriously concerned about something their child has done or failed to do or thinks. A couple of years ago I suspected that my son had done something of which I very much disapproved and this caused me a great deal of worry. The feeling of seeing him apparently go astray was devastating. Thank God, it turned out it wasn't half as serious as I had thought, and the world went back to normal for me. But it got me thinking. As my son grows up, he becomes ever more independent of his parents, and ever more free to make his own choices. Some of them will be choices that will cause us heartache—not least, because they may also cause him heartache.

It is hard to look on and see your beloved child make mistakes that may have harmful effects on its life. It is still absolutely necessary to let go and to let your children take risks, especially as they grow into their own identity. A child who is always kept on a short rein will not feel much love for its parents nor will it grow into a loving and responsible adult. Every life skill, including righteousness, takes practice, and practice involves making mistakes.

Is it the same for God, watching us as we bumble our way through the life God has given us? God chose in the very beginning to give us freedom. Without freedom, we cannot love God truly, nor our neighbour truly: coerced love is not true love, as you will know if you are familiar with the story of King Lear. Cordelia, Lear's youngest and best loved daughter, refuses to compete with her sisters in fulsome verbal expressions of love for her father—she simply says she loves him. That is the root of the tragedy that unfolds, for her father does not recognise that her simply stated love is true while her sisters are merely out for themselves and their expressions of love are merely a response to King Lear's request for them. Finally, too late, he realises that the love of his daughters is not something he can command but something that has to be freely given.

We, too, have to give our children freedom, but their use of it may cause us distress. Perhaps my pain at believing my son had done something I wouldn't want him to do is only a pale reflection of the pain God feels, as God watches us treat people as commodities, impoverish our neighbours, kill in God's name and trash the beautiful planet God has given us. (I'm not saying all of us do this, just that the human race collectively does these things.) In many ways, the human race is in its 'adolescent' phase, learning to take control of the world but not yet mature enough to manage it justly. We must be a great trial to God, yet still God lets us go our own way, only making it clear that we can always come home whenever we need to.

When I believed John had done something wrong, I didn't feel any anger against him, just sadness that he had got involved in something that was potentially harmful to him and others. As Christians we tend to emphasise God's anger against sin. In her visions, Julian of Norwich said, 'I saw no kind of wrath in God... the wrath is in ourselves.'[3] Could our idea that God is angry be a projection of the anger in ourselves at failing to meet our own standards?

Don't get me wrong: I do believe God gets angry, and the Bible states this very clearly. Perhaps the anger is not with individuals, however, but with injustice, corruption, exploitation. Perhaps God is the only one who can truly hate the sin and love the sinner—when we use this phrase about ourselves we are too often using it as an excuse for excluding and despising people.

Author Walter Wangerin tells a story about his adopted son. When the boy was a young teenager, his father was forced, against all his principles, to punish him physically for stealing. Once the boy was grown up, he recalled this incident and how it had helped to turn his life around. 'But it wasn't the smack that did it,' he explained, 'it was the fact that you cried when you smacked me.'[4] If we could really see God's pain when we don't live God's way, wouldn't we be far more moved by God's tears than by any thunderbolt from heaven?

Values

John was born into, and has grown up in, a church in which how we live and follow Jesus is considered as important as what we believe and how we worship. We have never imposed our faith on him, but he has always been surrounded by people whose values were very clear: values of care for the weakest, of standing up for justice, of faithfulness and commitment to each other.

Now he is a teenager, he has chosen not to come to church with us any more, although for some reason he still comes to church lunches! It's understandable—there are no other teenagers in the church, except his best friend who is now at boarding school and so isn't at church very often. (In fact, at the moment there are no children of any age in the church.)

Nevertheless, I see very often that he has absorbed our values and respects them. (I see this particularly in his comments on the television news.) I pray that one day he will encounter God for himself, possibly in a Christian setting quite different from our little Mennonite congregation.

Some parents bring up their children to pray daily and read the Bible from an early age. Some even encourage them to 'accept Jesus' at a very early age. I have always been a bit dubious about that approach—it seems to me it is just as likely to put them off religion in later life, as to bring them to a mature faith. Our denomination, which does not baptise babies, regards following Jesus as an adult commitment, which should be made only when we are capable of counting the cost of discipleship, as Jesus himself indicated:

'Whoever does not carry the cross and follow me cannot be my disciple. For which of you, intending to build a tower, does not first sit down and estimate the cost, to see whether he has enough to complete it?' (Luke 14:27–28)

Of course I sometimes have doubts about our 'hands off' approach to teaching our child about our faith. Unfortunately, it's too late now to adopt another policy! I do note, however, that God's approach to us as God's children is fairly 'hands off'. God does not immediately strike us down when we disobey God's commands or fail to be Christ-like.

One of the jobs of the church, as well as of parents, is to impart both love of God and adherence to godly values. However, just as a parent has to allow their child to question and weigh up the values of its parents, so I feel strongly that the job of a church leader or preacher is not to tell the congregation what to think. It is to teach them *how* to think, to engage with the scriptures for themselves, to evolve a God-centred mind. Despite the fact that the Bible often calls the godly community 'sheep', this does not mean we should follow blindly whatever shepherd God has put in charge of us. There are good and bad shepherds, and sheep have to learn to tell the voice of the good shepherd:

The one who enters by the gate is the shepherd of the sheep. The gatekeeper opens the gate for him, and the sheep hear his voice. He calls his own sheep by name and leads them out. When he has brought out all his own, he goes ahead of them, and the sheep follow him because they know his voice. They will not follow a stranger, but they will run from him because they do not know the voice of strangers. (John 10:2–5)

Matches

I heard a report on the radio of a child saying to its mother, 'Mummy, when you're dead I want to play with matches.' It struck me as a marvellous summing up of the human condition. Our parent God wants to protect us from things that would be harmful for us. Because they are prohibited, these are the very things we want to do most. We wish God dead, so that we can do as we like. At some deep level, perhaps we know that playing with matches will not be to our benefit but we want to do it anyway.

The conservative Amish communities in the USA have a period known in their Low German dialect as *Rumspringa*—literally 'jumping around'. Starting at the age of 16, teenagers are free from the rules and regulations, the strict dress code and the Christian commitment of the community. Some (mainly the boys) get cars, which the Amish do not use, and drive around dangerously fast. They may go on dates or indulge in too much alcohol.

The Amish, with their old-fashioned ways, are perennially fascinating to the 'modern' world. A while back there was a TV programme in which five Amish teenagers, in their *Rumspringa* period, came to the UK to stay with various families of different sorts in different areas, from a single-parent family on a council estate to landed gentry on a very different sort of estate. It was intriguing and sometimes moving to see how they responded to encountering the lives of modern teenagers, and how they were weighing up their Amish background and evaluating what was best in it. They were shocked by some of what they saw and heard, but they also treated the non-Amish kids with real respect and a listening attitude. Meanwhile some of the UK teenagers were very impressed by the Amish kids' ability to sew a dress, build a rabbit hutch and plant vegetables.

At the end of *Rumspringa*, which is a movable feast and can go on for several years, the Amish teenager has to decide whether to be baptised and join the tradition in which they have grown up. The vast majority, over 90 per cent, choose to become Amish and enjoy the benefits of a secure and God-centred lifestyle.

I think the Amish are very wise to allow their children a period of 'playing with matches'. I am also sure that, like all Christian parents, they spend a lot of time praying that their teenagers don't get burned.

Loss

Being a parent is in some ways a continual process of loss. To have a toddler you must lose a baby, to have a school child you must lose a preschool child, and when you suddenly find you have a spotty, grumpy 'monster' with legs so long that he doesn't know where to put them, you may find yourself thinking, 'Whatever happened to that gorgeous little child I used to have?' I haven't yet got to the stage of seeing my chick fly the nest (it still seems almost unattainable) but I clearly remember that on his first day of school, it was me who cried, not him! The first time I let him go alone to the corner shop, I was terrified that he wouldn't look when he crossed the road. That was nothing compared to the first time I let him go on his own on the Tube to central London, even though it was a journey he had done many times with his father, and he was meeting his best friend's father at the other end. As soon as you hand your baby over to someone else to hold, the letting go process begins. After that, life is a long series of letting go as your children acquire new skills and new independence. For those of us with children who are taking a bit longer to mature in some areas, or perhaps children who will never be fully independent, the temptation is to be more protective than the average parent. Our children are so much more vulnerable and their understanding of the outside world may be limited. Yet even if we have 'special' children, the time comes when we have to let go, if only letting them go into someone else's care for a while.

If our parenting is the sort that supervises every move (and occasionally it has to be), it is not surprising if we cast God in the same mould, believing that God wants us to be completely passive and go only where God has explicitly told us to. In fact, even the least able children deserve some life separate from their parents—and perhaps we can take our cue from God who gives us freedom to make our own choices. The God I see in Jesus is the God who lets God's children go—and also the one who welcomes us back again. May we have the same freeing—and welcoming—attitude to our own children.

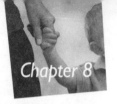

Chapter 8

Making plans

When I grow up

When John was small he used to play a game of 'growing up', which basically consisted of him asking, 'What comes next?' He would say, for example, 'What will I be after I'm a child?' and the answer would be 'a teenager'. Then we would go through his going to secondary school, going into sixth form, leaving school, going to college, getting a job, getting married and having his own children. It seemed to make him feel secure knowing what was coming next (this is often true of children on the autistic spectrum), and perhaps it made him feel powerful as he imagined himself as an adult.

Of course, things don't always work out quite as planned! Right now he's repeating the first term of sixth form, a year after he first tried, and we still have two years until he can boast some A levels.

As a young Christian I was taught about something called 'guidance'. Apparently, at least as it was taught to me, God set out a series of clues rather like a treasure hunt, and you had to spot them to find out what God wants for your life. If you failed to get the right answer, then you were on the wrong path and your life was out of God's will. I was often given Isaiah 30:21, which I now like to call the first appearance of satnav in the Bible: 'And when you turn to the right or when you turn to the left, your ears shall hear a voice behind you, saying, "This is the way; walk in it."'

God's GPS? Maybe, but notice that the word from behind doesn't come as you stand still and wait for it: it comes 'when you turn to the right or the left'. We don't get guided as we sit still and wait for a sign but as we keep walking in the light of Christ.

I also often heard or read in tracts, 'God loves you and has a wonderful plan for your life.' (This was rapidly corrupted by us single women into, 'God loves you and has a wonderful man for your life'!) It gave me the impression that my entire life was mapped out ahead of me by God and that all I had to do was work out what God had in store.

No doubt this was an interpretation of Psalm 139:16: 'In your book were written all the days that were formed for me, when none of them as yet existed.' That is not the only way to interpret this verse, and increasingly I feel it was a wrong one. Imagine a parent who had a child and then mapped out the child's entire life from the word 'Go', determining who their friends would be, what they would study, who they would marry and what job they would have, all in the smallest detail. Surely such a parent would be a monster, not a model parent? In the late 1970s the group XTC released a hit song called 'Making plans for Nigel', in which Nigel's parents declared repeatedly, 'He has this future in British Steel.' The song was not exactly recommending the parents' attitude, and I don't think British Steel would have got a very willing or committed employee.

A child with such parents would certainly be right to rebel against them and do everything opposite to what they had planned. Is this the sort of parent God is? Does God really plan every detail of our lives before we have even started living them? Do we have to figure out a set of clues to make sure we are on the path God has preordained for us?

I had a dear friend who died of cancer in her late 50s (after her husband and 20-year-old daughter also died of cancer within a few years of each other). She used to say to people that she had not yet worked out what she wanted to do when she grew up. Yet she had a variety of socially very useful jobs, was a shining example of faith to others, and used her considerable talents in many ways. Was there some master plan that she missed out on through not being attentive enough to God's guidance? I personally don't think so.

Early in her life, as a young Christian, she had a non-Christian boyfriend and was about to give him up when he unexpectedly became a Christian. She thought this meant she should marry him, but the marriage was a total disaster and didn't even last two years. She thought she had been guided, but in fact she had failed to take into account her boyfriend's youth and immaturity, which didn't disappear the moment he became a Christian (not to mention her own youth and immaturity).

Later, she lived with another non-Christian and had two children. It wasn't until he had his first bout of cancer that he consented to get married. He attended our church faithfully for 18 years and was very much part of the community, and at last he requested baptism on his deathbed. Did God guide her into her second marriage? It was certainly a happy one, although it sadly ended with her husband's death—but also with his coming to faith.

I no longer think that God's guidance is all that simple. If we as parents tried to plan our children's entire lives, our children would in effect never become adults but would be perpetually dependent on our decisions. Perhaps if God planned out every detail of our lives, we would never become mature Christians, able to make decisions based on the law of love which has been written on our hearts (see Hebrews 10:8).

For us as parents, it is a lot more important that children have our values 'written on their hearts' than that they do everything we expect or hope for them to do. They are born to live their own lives, not ours. The fact that a mother has always longed to be a ballet dancer does not mean she should put her daughter through ballet school, for example. I think it's somewhat the same with God: God does not use God's children to live out a prescribed life but sets us free to be ourselves, which are, of course, the selves God created us to be.

Whatever

'Wait a minute!' you may be saying. 'Surely God has a "best way" for us; surely God is involved in the details of our lives and shows us the direction to go in?' I certainly believe God is involved in the details of our lives—but that doesn't mean every detail is preordained.

If I ask my mother, 'Which looks better, the green scarf or the blue?', I expect her to give me an answer, but I also expect to be able to make my own choice, which may not be the same as hers. She probably won't mind which I choose, as long as I wear a scarf. (Since being a mother myself, I have learned the importance of getting your child to wear a scarf.)

Suppose God doesn't care whether you end up as a godly social worker or a godly plumber, as long as you do your best work and do it knowing that God can work through you? Maybe it doesn't matter to God whether you say 'Yes' or 'No' to that man who's asking you to marry him—because God will use you and bless your life whichever way you go.

When I read the Bible I see a God who uses the broken, the confused, the flawed and even the rebellious. Consider this passage from Jeremiah:

The word that came to Jeremiah from the Lord: 'Come, go down to the potter's house, and there I will let you hear my words.' So I went down to the potter's house, and there he was working at his wheel. The vessel he was making of clay was spoiled in the potter's hand, and he reworked it into another vessel, as seemed good to him. (18:1–4)

Here we see God responding to something that didn't go according to plan, and making God's will happen in spite of the flaw that has appeared in the 'clay'. Not only that, but I believe that God actually uses our 'flaws' to make something that would never have been possible if we hadn't gone astray or made a mistake.

The philosopher Kierkegaard had a strange belief that events repeat themselves in our lives, as though God is giving us a second chance. I can certainly see this happening at some crucial points in my life. For instance, at university I had a steady boyfriend who was very kind to me but whom I wasn't in love with (sorry, David, if you ever read this book). After two years I finished with him in a not very nice way, by going off with one of his best friends (sorry again, David…). Many years later, I found myself again with a boyfriend who was not at all what I would have chosen for myself, but in this case I had a very strong feeling that God was leading me into this relationship. I have now been married to him for 22 years!

If I had married David, I would have missed all the painful years of being single, and perhaps I would have been happy.

Maybe I took a wrong step in not marrying him—but God was well able to redeem the situation and gave me another chance to marry sensibly. Certainly, if I had married any of the many unsuitable men I had fallen in love with over the years, I think I would have had a much more difficult life.

As parents, we feel pain when we see our children making choices we can see are not good for them. Yet we must let them make those choices. If we are patient, we may live to see them on a better path. And God is the most patient parent there is.

Parental guidance

Does all this mean that God doesn't actually guide us at all? Far from it. Children, even when they've grown up, still need guidance from their parents. As they grow they will (eventually) come to value the wisdom of their parents who have, after all, lived longer than the children have and have (we hope) acquired more wisdom and knowledge of the world. An old joke goes like this: 'When I was a boy of 14, my father was so ignorant I could hardly stand to have the old man around. But when I got to be 21, I was astonished at how much the old man had learned in seven years' (attributed to Mark Twain). In normal circumstances a grown child, if they have been parented well, will continue to turn to their parents for advice (as well as money).

The key is in being asked. All too often parents (and I am just as guilty here) are far too ready to give advice and guidance even when they are not asked for it. Children can quite rightly resent this as they want to make their own way in the world. I still have issues, which I probably should have outgrown, with my mother giving me unsolicited advice. To be fair, it was she who told me the following joke: 'What's the difference between a Jewish mother and a Rottweiler? The Rottweiler eventually lets go.'

I have to recognise that I am a Jewish mother, too, and my son frequently has to tell me off for offering him advice or information that he neither wants nor needs. I am gradually learning, I hope, to wait until I am asked.

Sometimes, I think, God waits until we ask for guidance. There are also times when God quite clearly steps in and prevents us doing something stupid, or 'arranges' things for us when we are too weak to work it out ourselves. I have had a few dramatic occasions like this in my life, when the path ahead was pointed out absolutely unambiguously. These occurrences are rare, and most of the time I have to go ahead in the dark, hoping that if I take a wrong step, God will redeem it. This doesn't mean I am getting no guidance from God—it may mean that God is guiding me through circumstances instead rather than in recognisable 'signs'. As I said on my Facebook status recently, 'All I know is that when I pray, more coincidences happen.' Perhaps God as a loving parent is giving me opportunities rather than suggestions.

Even when our parents are dead, as my father now is, we come to a point when we can stop and say to ourselves, 'What would my father/mother (or other parental figure) say or do about this?' We have 'internalised' our parents and their ideas now influence us, often without our even knowing it.

Similarly, for many Christians, 'What would Jesus do?' is still a useful question, although it has its limits (we can only guess, in the end, what Jesus would do about, for example, the plea for same-sex marriage, since he said nothing at all on the subject). Perhaps 'What does God think about this?' is a more useful question, since we have a great deal of thinking about what God thinks in the Bible. This, however, is more useful for general moral guidance than for specific decisions about which way our lives should go; in the latter, we often have to rely on our, hopefully God-influenced, gut feelings. As I have said, I believe God will lead us, whatever path we choose, perhaps even despite our choices.

No torture

I don't believe that God predestines every moment of our human lives. What about our eternal destiny, though? Many Christians (although not all) believe that the vast majority of humankind is destined to be doomed to eternal punishment, and only those who have made a Christian commitment and kept to it will be saved. Some even believe that whether we go to heaven or hell is decided long before we are even born. Let me put it this way: what kind of parent would arbitrarily choose a minority of her children to be especially favoured and allocate the rest to eternal torture? Not a loving parent, surely, but an abuser comparable to the man (an Austrian, I am ashamed to say) who kept his daughter in a locked basement for 18 years and fathered seven children by her. Or indeed to Hitler (also an Austrian) who decided that entire categories of people, not just Jews but also homosexuals, Romas and those with physical or learning disabilities, should be wiped out. In a world where torture is getting less and less acceptable, and capital punishment is outlawed in most democratic countries, how do we expect people to want to ally themselves with a God who is presented to them like that?

Here is what a post on the website Ship of Fools (www. ship-of-fools.com) said about being a parent:

If I had ever believed in hell, it would have stopped the moment I became a parent. I cannot conceive of disowning my child, whatever she might do, in any circumstances, for one second, ever. God's love for us is not less than our love for our children.

I find it impossible to conceive of a God who is an infinitely loving parent, yet who could create millions of people throughout history who were destined from the beginning to be destroyed, let alone eternally tortured. That kind of God would be a monster.

I do believe, reluctantly, in some form of hell, since Jesus spoke about it quite often. In order to give us freedom, God has made a world in which some people will not choose the way of Jesus. I do not for a moment believe that such people will be tormented by demons for ever, in some kind of disembodied state in which it is still possible to feel pain— and I do not believe the Bible teaches this.

Think about it: if there is an eternal 'place' or state in which the vast majority of humankind are to be eternally tormented, then there is eternally a large part of the creation where things are not as God wishes. God's desire is to be 'all in all', as Paul puts it in 1 Corinthians:

The last enemy to be destroyed is death. For 'God has put all things in subjection under his feet.' ... When all things are subjected to him, then the Son himself will also be subjected to the one who put all things in subjection under him, so that God may be all in all. (15:26–28)

In Colossians, Paul tells us that God is in the reclamation business, not just for a small number of people, but for 'all things': 'Through him God was pleased to reconcile to himself all things, whether on earth or in heaven, by making

132

peace through the blood of his cross' (1:20). If God's plan is to reconcile all things, how can there be, for eternity, a corner of reality where nothing is reconciled and everything is hostile?

This is what I think the Bible does teach, and an increasing number of people are coming to this view: that at the coming again of Jesus all evil will be destroyed, and those who have chosen evil will also be destroyed. This is the 'annihilation' theory of hell, in which hell itself is ultimately destroyed. This is the view of many evangelical scholars; and there is a lot of evidence for it in the Bible, which I don't have space to go into here, but try searching it out for yourself—there are several good books on the market that deal with this theory.[1] (Let us also remember that all our theology is composed of theories, because God's reality is a mystery.)

Many or few?

Now I can hear you quoting, 'The gate is narrow and the road is hard that leads to life, and there are few who find it' (Matthew 7:14). It does look, doesn't it, as though Jesus is saying only a minority will be saved. Actually, I think Jesus is talking here about the cost of discipleship, which few want to take on—this is nothing to do with God condemning millions to hell. By contrast, Jesus tells us in his parable of the great feast, 'I tell you, many will come from east and west and will eat with Abraham and Isaac and Jacob in the kingdom of heaven' (Matthew 8:11). Here he prophesies that many who thought they were outside the favoured people of God will in fact joyfully come to the feast Jesus will hold at the end of time and in context it is clear that this 'many' are Gentiles, strangers to the Jewish law.

It's true that he goes on to say that 'the heirs of the kingdom will be thrown into the outer darkness, where there will be weeping and gnashing of teeth' (v. 12). This is saying, I believe, not that many will be condemned, but in fact the exact opposite: that the self-styled 'few', those who think of themselves as 'the faithful remnant', will be thrown out of the feast (although there is no hint that the weeping and gnashing are eternal, but it is simply saying that they will be outside and that this will cause them pain).

Notice, too, that in John's Gospel, Jesus implies that people are divided into those who choose darkness and those who choose light, not on the basis just of what they believe, but of how they live their lives:

And this is the judgment, that the light has come into the world, and people loved darkness rather than light because their deeds were evil. For all who do evil hate the light and do not come to the light, so that their deeds may not be exposed. But those who do what is true come to the light, so that it may be clearly seen that their deeds have been done in God. (John 3:19–21)

This is backed up by Matthew 25:31–46, the parable of the sheep and goats, where Jesus judges the nations (not individuals) by how they have served those in need.

Jesus seems to be saying that people who love goodness and truth, and let this love affect their lives, will be the ones who recognise him as redeemer. Whether or not they have understood *The Four Spiritual Laws* (as in a booklet by Bill Bright, founder of Campus Crusade for Christ) or said 'the sinner's prayer' is not in view here. It is more a case of what a person's basic life orientation is, whether they choose to love good and hate evil, or the other way around. Those who love good will know who Jesus is when they meet him and will welcome him.

We know that there are millions of people in the world who have not heard of Jesus, or only heard of him in a form distorted by cultural accommodation, a form they have rightly rejected because the Jesus they heard of did not seem to be on the side of justice. Do we really have to believe that all those people are automatically condemned? I no longer believe (actually, I don't think I ever did) in a God who is so hard to access that there is only one right way of being aligned with God's purposes. I believe that those who 'naturally' do the right thing and live the right way will know Jesus at his Second Coming, and will cast themselves on his mercy. And I think I have the apostle Paul on my side:

All who have sinned apart from the law will also perish apart from the law, and all who have sinned under the law will be judged by the law. For it is not the hearers of the law who are righteous in God's sight, but the doers of the law who will be justified. When Gentiles, who do not possess the law, do instinctively what the law requires, these, though not having the law, are a law to themselves. They show that what the law requires is written on their hearts, to which their own conscience also bears witness; and their conflicting thoughts will accuse or perhaps excuse them on the day when, according to my gospel, God, through Jesus Christ, will judge the secret thoughts of all. (Romans 2:12–16)

This doesn't appear to say that only those who call themselves 'Christian' will be saved. Does this make it not worth being a Christian? Far from it, for when we do recognise God in Christ, we cannot turn away and ignore him—we have to respond. It does suggest that salvation is not a big game of

'Simon says', with only those who can say the right formula allowed to stay in the game.

I simply don't think it's possible to believe in God as an infinitely loving parent, who, if anything, loves us more when we are trapped in the pit of sin or despair, and at the same time believe that God destines the vast majority of God's children to destruction. Well, I guess it is possible, since many people do believe it, but I don't think it is logical.

I knew that

If neither the course of our lives nor our eternal destiny is mapped out by God from all eternity, then what about God's foreknowledge? Surely God knows everything we have done or will ever do, since God is all-knowing? Doesn't this amount to God's planning everything we ever do and everything that happens to us?

Trained theologians, of which I am not one, have pondered and deliberated and held forth on these questions for millennia, so I don't pretend to be able to solve it in this one little chapter. I just want to suggest something. I've been married for 22 years and a mother for 17. Believe it or not, I've known my son since before he was born. So I can often predict exactly what he will say or do. Take a plate of biscuits (please take them, I'm trying to diet). If I offer John some assorted biscuits, which happens to include his favourite type (Café Noir), I can predict with 99 per cent accuracy which biscuit he will take. I am his mother, after all.

Does that mean I made him take that particular biscuit? Certainly not. The most I've done is to arrange things so that it's likely he'll take one particular biscuit, by putting a Café Noir biscuit in the selection. I've put a choice before him, and it's always possible that he'll confound my expectations and take a completely different biscuit, maybe one of those so-called 'squashed fly biscuits'. At least, it would be possible if I ever bought those, which I don't.

If God is a parent, then it follows that God has extremely detailed knowledge of all God's children—in fact, God knows them better than they know themselves. It's hardly surprising, then, that God is likely to know what we are going to do. It doesn't follow that God is operating us like string puppets, determining every little move we make.

What if God, although all-knowing and all-powerful, has chosen to live within self-imposed limits and not exercise that knowledge and power? The spiritual writer David Runcorn, in his wonderful book *Choice, Desire and the Will of God*,[2] has included a 'letter to God', which I first heard him deliver in a talk at the Lee Abbey Christian conference centre in Devon. This is how it begins:

Dear God,

I don't often sit down and write to you. But there's a difficult question that I want to ask. It's bothered me for a while now and it's this: Do you really know everything—absolutely every-thing? You see, I can't help feeling disappointed if you do. And (forgive me if this sounds disrespectful), I can't help feeling you are missing something if you do. Take surprises, for example. You can never be surprised... But that's an awful thought to me. Have you really never experienced a moment completely unexpected—the delicious thrill of a complete surprise—a gift of love and fun that was kept a secret though we nearly burst?

And this is how the letter ends:

Sometimes, in a playful mood, I want to creep up quietly behind you and suddenly burst upon you with my loudest joy—and see you jump! ... But I can't if you know already. And it wouldn't be the same if I thought you were just pretending for me. And so I have a fear inside. I'm afraid that if you know everything, you must be rather serious.

Ever yours,
Guess who?

Runcorn does not come to any binding conclusions about God's omniscience and whether we can surprise God. As I said, the best theologians throughout history have been baffled by this. David Runcorn does, however, suggest that God acts within voluntarily chosen limits, for the sake of love for God's creatures, and in order to create a world in which there is freedom. Love inevitably places limits on our lives and choices, and perhaps parental love places more limits than any other kind of love. Could it be that God, because God has chosen freely to love us, also chooses to limit God's own knowledge of what we are going to do?

Being surprised by one's children is one of the greatest joys of parenthood. The other day I laughed my head off when my son said to me, as he was on his way to bed, 'Before I go I'm just going to leave you in suspense about...' and then just stopped. I love his sense of humour! I also still laugh about the time, when he was smaller, and when, walking up the stairs behind me, he pronounced, 'It's not me, it's someone else.' This strikes me as very like David Runcorn's wish to creep up behind God and make God jump. Even if it can't be done, it's worth a try.

As its creator, God must know a great deal more about the physical world and how it works than we do. When we make a new scientific discovery, say about subatomic particles, it is something that God already knew from the beginning. But God has also put unlimited creativity in the human race and given us freedom to exercise it. Might God, then, sometimes look at the world and think, 'Gosh! I didn't know Picasso was going to paint like that!' or 'I'm so proud of that new way of dancing my children have just invented'? Surely God, like us human parents, can rejoice in the ever unpredictable ways in which we grow as human beings and as God's children? I like to think so, anyway.

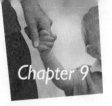

Chapter 9

The pain of love

After all I've done

When I was studying English literature at university, I discovered a type of medieval poem that portrayed Jesus hanging on the cross, calling out to everyone who passes by to look and see what they have done to him, and what he has endured for them. It was based on Lamentations 1:12:

Is it nothing to you, all you who pass by?
Look and see
if there is any sorrow like my sorrow
which was brought upon me,
which the Lord inflicted
on the day of his fierce anger.

This is actually about the destruction of Jerusalem but, like many Old Testament passages, it was seen by medieval scholars as a prefiguring of Christ. I always felt a little uncomfortable with this vision: it smacked to me too much of the parent who asks a child—sometimes an already grown-up child—'How can you do that/say that after all I've done for you?' The child, quite understandably, sometimes answers, 'I didn't ask to be born!'

Parents do indeed make many sacrifices for their children: sacrifices of time, emotion, even money. (Perhaps especially money! Childrearing doesn't come cheap these days, especially in well-off countries). To choose (and not everyone chooses, or is able) to be a parent is to open oneself to all kinds of heartache as well as a great deal of often extremely boring and repetitive work. I don't believe parents should place heavy expectations on their children, either to fulfil the parents' own dreams or to be consumed with gratitude for all the parents have done. After all, it is quite true that the children didn't ask to be born. When it comes to the crunch, we don't really have children for their benefit; we have them for ours, because we want a family. My longing to have a child was for entirely selfish reasons—I wanted my 'line' to carry on, and I wanted to be a 'proper' family. Thankfully, having to care for a child, especially one with special needs, very rapidly teaches one to think of others and their needs, otherwise one would give up immediately!

I don't believe in a God who says to us, 'You'd better do what I want after all I've done for you.' Loving God out of a sense of duty would not be the sort of love God wants, I believe (nor is it the sort of love earthly parents want). True love, whether of God or of others, must be freely and joyfully given.

Thinking about sacrifice leads me inevitably back to Jesus' death on the cross. There has been a lot of debate in recent years about the so-called penal substitution theory of the atonement, in which an angry God demands a penalty for human sin, and Jesus steps into the breach and pays the price we were unable to pay. Now I know a lot of people get great comfort from this understanding of Jesus' paying for our sins, but it has never meant much to me, although the cross itself means a great deal to me..I have sometimes wondered whether people relate to this picture of the cross better if they grew up in a family where rules, reward and punishment were strong elements. This was very much not the case for me, so I don't have such a strong sense that 'every sin has to be paid for'.

What I, and many others, find difficult with this penal view of the cross is that you end up with one 'part' of God (if I can speak somewhat crudely of the Trinity), satisfying his anger by punishing another part of God. In fact, what you get is a father punishing the 'eldest son' for the misdemeanours of the rest of the family! This doesn't strike me as a very good model of parenting. It also posits a God who is essentially violent and who visits that violence on his son, which is problematic for those of us who believe being a Christian calls us to non-violence.

I don't entirely understand the cross—who does? It's a mystery. What makes better sense for me is the biblical view that 'in Christ God was reconciling the world to himself' (2 Corinthians 5:19). In other words, God the father was as involved as God the son in the pain and sorrow of bearing the consequences of our sinfulness. This may well be a heresy called patripassianism, but in that case I'm happy to be a heretic. Fortunately for me, we are saved by grace through faith, not by correct doctrine.

In terms of a parent–child relationship, at the very least we can be sure that a parent experiencing the death of their only and beloved child would feel and identify with their child's pain in such a way that they felt pretty much the same pain as their child was feeling. Indeed, most parents would wish they could die instead of their child. Witness the grief of King David mourning the loss of his dear son Absalom: 'O my son Absalom, my son, my son Absalom! Would I had died instead of you, O Absalom, my son, my son!' (2 Samuel 18:33).

Having witnessed my parents' grief at my brother's suicide —and I know it never, ever goes away—I can identify strongly with this emotion.

For me, the cross is not so much about punishment and making good as it is about God's identifying with us, taking the whole of the wrongs and suffering of the world into God's own self, and bearing the pain, sorrow and shame of it all. I don't fully understand how this 'works'—as I said, it's a mystery. The resurrection shows us that, paradoxically, this apparent defeat of God turns into the greatest victory over the powers that hold us bound. I can see just a little of that reflected in the much smaller sacrifices that I have to make as a parent.

This view also gives us a non-violent God who, in Jesus, demonstrates that it is better to suffer violence than to inflict it, and that our suffering of violence can, in some unfathomable way, be redemptive. Some theologians call the penal view of the cross 'the myth of redemptive violence' and believe it shapes our society in all sorts of negative ways, making us accept war and other violence. I tend to agree with them, and prefer to believe in 'the truth of redemptive suffering'.

Daily denial

What about our call to imitate Jesus, to take up our own cross daily and deny ourselves? Jesus said, 'No one has greater love than this, to lay down one's life for one's friends' (John 15:13).

Surely Paul echoes this when he tells husbands, 'Husbands, love your wives, just as Christ loved the church and gave himself up for her' (Ephesians 5:25). This suggests that a husband should 'lay down his life' for his wife, as Christ laid down his life for us.

Many years ago I did a brief experiment, asking friends what they thought this meant. Without exception, the men said it meant that a husband should be willing to die to save his wife in an emergency. The women, by contrast, said they thought it meant a daily, unspectacular laying down of one's own needs and desires for the sake of one's partner. It strikes me that the men's version commits them only to something which, in most cases, is very unlikely to happen—whereas the women's version demands an attitude of sacrifice every day! Rather convenient for the men...

In parenthood, too, we are, in normal circumstances, unlikely to have to die so that our child can live. However, we are all required to make the daily, wearing choices that put our child's needs ahead of our own, whether it's broken nights or trying to get your teenager to do her homework. That is certainly a lesson in taking up one's cross and denying oneself. It is an even greater sacrifice for those parents whose 'special' child will never actually be independent. They will have to be 'hands-on' parents for the whole of their lives, and to take incredibly difficult decisions about who cares for their child after they have died.

I think the significance of Jesus' death is about much more than what happened one Friday at the beginning of Passover in AD33. I think it shows us something eternal about the character of God's 'parenthood': that God is a parent who, throughout the whole of history, has been willing to bear our pain and corruptness, to save us from bearing them. As I said earlier, from God's viewpoint we are all 'special' children— children who are in some way damaged or incapable—which means God's task of caring for us never ends. God has to care for us for eternity. That's simply what a good parent does. And that's a God I want to follow.

Parenting and pain

To become a parent is to become 'a hostage to fortune', to open oneself to pain that may be much more than we had ever anticipated. I think of a woman who was at college with me, whose daughter, after having just gained a first in her degree, was killed in a car crash some years ago. I think of the mother with a severely autistic son who will never learn to talk to her but just makes incoherent noises. Not everyone endures such deep pain in their parenthood, of course, but what about the daughter who marries someone her parents think is really bad for her? What about the son who leaves the Christian sect in which you have so carefully brought him up, and apparently rejects all you have taught him? (My husband was that son!)

My mother used to refer ruefully to a sign in our local variety theatre, which read: 'All children must be paid for'. (Being one of her children, I was none too pleased about how she interpreted this!) Of course, parenthood is full of joy as well as pain, but it is never an easy ride. Occasionally, I hear a mother saying of her child, 'She never gave me a moment's worry in her life.' This worries me. I wonder whether that parent really doesn't care much, or whether the child is so suppressed and conformed to its parents' requirements that it is hardly a separate being at all. Worry isn't the same as love (although my own mother seems to think it is), but if you love anyone or anything at all, you lay yourself open to the risk of losing that person or thing, or seeing it damaged beyond repair. All parents worry at some time, if they really know what it means to be a parent.

This is beautifully expressed in the 'children's story for grown-ups', *The Little Prince* by Antoine de Saint-Exupéry.[1]

The little prince, from a tiny unknown planet, loves a rose, which is the only flower that grows on his planet. Here he tries to explain to the grounded aviator, whom he has met in the desert, what the flower means to him (the aviator has drawn a sheep for the boy, as he wants a sheep to keep the planet's baobab trees from growing tall):

If someone loves a flower of which just one example exists among all the millions and millions of stars, that's enough to make him happy when he looks at the stars. He tells himself, 'My flower's up there somewhere…' But if the sheep eats the flower, then for him it's as if, suddenly, all the stars went out. And that isn't important?

For the prince, the thought that his flower may be eaten by the sheep is the most terrifying thought in the world. Later the prince meets a fox who teaches him to tame it, and then leaves:

'Goodbye,' said the fox. 'Here is my secret. It's quite simple: One sees clearly only with the heart. Anything essential is invisible to the eyes… It's the time that you spent on your rose that makes your rose so important… People have forgotten this truth,' the fox said, 'But you mustn't forget it. You become responsible for what you've tamed. You're responsible for your rose.'

Rearing a child is like taming that fox: a process of teaching the 'little alien' or apprentice human being how to relate to other human beings and so become a full human person. For most parents, the initial period—say, the first 18 years—when you have done your best to help your child face the world, comes to an end. Being a parent goes on for the rest of your life, however, because 'you become responsible for what you've tamed'. Your relationship may change, but your child will never cease to be your child.

Is it like this with God, too? The process of God's 'taming' us may go on for many years; it probably goes on for our whole lives. This doesn't mean we have to remain dependent and helpless. We have seen already that God wants us to mature and to grow 'to the full stature of Christ' (Ephesians 4:13). We are meant to grow into a Christ-like way of being, which will form our responses, without having to check 'the rules' all the time. When the law of love is written on our hearts, we can act spontaneously from our 'Christian instincts', as a result of what Mennonite theologian Alan Kreider calls 're-reflexing'.

I knew as soon as John was born that he was physically 'the image of' his father, but now as he grows I see all sorts of other ways in which he is both like Ed and like me, and it's impossible to say what's due to his genetic heritage, and what to the ways in which we have tried as his parents to inform and influence him. There are already some things we don't need to tell him anymore because he's taken them on board.

This by no means implies that a grown child ceases to need its parents. When I was single, I often rang my mother with the words, 'Is that the recipe service?' In reality, she is much more than a recipe service to me. I continue to have a relationship with her because I love her. God's children never reach a point of not needing God's help. It is the very Spirit of God within and among us that makes it possible for us to live in a Christ-like way, and we need to keep constantly in touch with God's Spirit.

In our society, families may live widely dispersed, hardly

communicating with each other. This is one of the reasons the Amish community does not use cars or telephones as these inventions make it too easy to leave the family and the community in which one has grown up. (I did notice when I was in America, however, that they had accepted trains.) In the society of Jesus' day, adult children were much more likely to be living with or near their parents or working in the family business (as indeed Jesus himself did). When Jesus tells parables about motherhood or fatherhood, this is the social situation he has in mind. In such a society, the prodigal son's request to have his inheritance now and leave his family was just about the most shocking thing you could conceivably say to your parent (see the story in Luke 15:11–32). It was tantamount to saying, 'I wish you were already dead.' (The only thing more shocking is the way the father welcomes the son back again when he comes home. It has even been suggested that this parable should really be called 'The prodigal father'.)

Prodigals

Although preaching and teaching on the parable of the prodigal son has tended to concentrate on the younger son, for the sake of the evangelistic opportunity this can give, those of us who are parents might find it interesting and fruitful to see ourselves in the parent. How do we deal with it when our own beloved child goes 'off to a far country', whether literally or metaphorically? I know a lovely Christian family, a minister's family in fact, whose younger son became a heroin addict in his late teens. I can only imagine how agonising that was for his parents. (As far as I know the son is all right now.) There are many families with one or more of the children estranged from their parents. Or what about the family who have a conservative view on homosexuality and then discover that their son or daughter is gay? Or the couple I know through the internet, whose estranged son has had 'gender reassignment' and is now their daughter?

Our experience of having 'prodigal children' lets us see a tiny glimpse of the pain God must feel at the way human society continues to propagate hatred and injustice, or simply to live in excessive affluence while others starve and die of easily preventable diseases. Sadly, too many of us (and we are all prone to this—I see it in myself) take the position of the elder brother, who is scandalised that a feast is given for his misbehaving sibling, and who resents the fact that he has always obeyed his father and has never been given such a feast. The elder brother was clearly meant to represent the religious authorities of the time, who were shocked that Jesus seemed to prefer to spend his time with 'sinners'. Surely the point of Jesus' parable is not only that God has a welcome for those who repent but also that we should model ourselves on the forgiving father rather than the jealous brother.

Most people who are literally fathers or mothers will happily take an erring child back, although there are those who say, 'Never darken my door again' and mean it. I believe that the church is called to be like the father in the parable, and be ready to welcome those already of our number who have fallen into gross sin but want to be cleansed as well as those coming in from outside with a dubious history. Unfortunately, church is not always a congenial place for people whose lives are chaotic or corrupted. It is so easy to slip into a culture of respectability and of belief in our own moral superiority. Becoming a Christian may not transform someone's lifestyle instantly (although it sometimes does):

they may still go on for a long time to have habits that annoy or worry other people. (Actually, we all have habits that annoy or worry other people, however long we've been Christians.)

The irony is that the elder brother, as the father makes clear, could have had any number of fatted calves and feasts with his friends, if he'd only asked. Clearly he didn't believe in his father's generosity and love, and thought the only way he could please his father was by working non-stop and never leaving the straight and narrow path.

Distorted images

Perhaps this is a good point at which to think about how children may view their parents, which is not always accurately. Certainly my son, being a teenager, is entirely convinced that we are the most embarrassing parents in the world, although this can't be true as I know of several other most embarrassing parents in the world living quite nearby!

Psychologically, children begin from a very early age to internalise images of their parents, which have a great role in their own growth and mental stability but which may also be quite distorted. For instance, I am still scared of my mother's criticism, yet I was astonished to hear the other day that she gets nervous about ringing me up! I really didn't think I was so unapproachable.

What is true of our attitudes to our own parents is all the more true of how we view God. Gerard Hughes' bestseller *God of Surprises*[2] pictures a child being told about Good Old Uncle George, and how knowledgeable, loving and kind he is; but also about Uncle George's dark and terrifying basement, with an ever-burning furnace, where he locks any relatives who don't do exactly what he says. Needless to say, the child who hears this becomes very ambivalent about whether it really wants to meet Good Old Uncle George.

Through inadequate or distorted teaching, or because of our own psychological make-up, we may have similarly odd views of God, seeing God not so much as an infinitely loving parent than as a disapproving authority figure whom it is extremely difficult to please. I constantly battle against this sort of image of God and struggle to have a more positive image of God—in fact, a more Jesus-like one (although Jesus himself can be quite scary at times).

This in turn may affect the way we go on to parent, and thus we will raise a new generation of kids who see God as an exacting tyrant and possibly want nothing at all to do with this God. Parenting sacrificially, as God parents us and loves us sacrificially, is a lot more costly. By 'parenting sacrificially' I don't mean letting your children run wild and do whatever they want. As I have learned from experience, constructive discipline can involve great sacrifice on the part of parents, especially if discipline doesn't come naturally.

Let's have a party

The parable of the prodigal son is, as the shorter parables around it are, not only a story of pain and loss. Primarily, it is a story about finding, about the joy of recovering what you thought would never be yours again. This is why the part about the elder brother is so sad. He is unable truly to hear it when his father says, 'We had to celebrate and rejoice, because this brother of yours was dead and has come to life; he was lost and has been found' (Luke 15:32). Notice how the father pointedly says 'this brother of yours' when the elder son has just criticised 'this son of yours', not acknowledging that he himself has a relationship with the lost and found younger son. Any fellow child of God is a sister or brother of mine, whether they know it or not, whether they act like one or not.

When we are worried about our children, especially when they have additional needs, it is easy to forget simply to enjoy them. Whenever John has achieved something we thought he might not be able to, we have been so proud of him and so glad we had him. He is, to use a biblical image, the apple of our eyes (Psalm 17:8). And so are we, of God's eyes. We just don't always know it, just as our own children don't always recognise how much we love them.

Whatever struggle you have had with your children, even if you have lost a child, as my parents did, I'll bet you don't wish that you had never had them. That includes the child that caused or still causes you most heartache. We saw in Chapter 1, in the story of Noah, how God apparently regretted having created humankind, but the story quickly goes on to show God's promising humanity a future. Here, a little later in the same story, God is renewing his relationship with humanity:

Then God said to Noah and to his sons with him, 'As for me, I am establishing my covenant with you and your descendants after you, and with every living creature that is with you, the birds, the domestic animals, and every animal of the earth with you, as many as came out of the ark. I establish my covenant with you, that never again shall all flesh be cut off by the waters of a flood, and never again shall there be a flood to destroy the earth.' (Genesis 9:8–11)

When I go through a crowded Tube station, I sometimes reflect that God must like people a great deal, since God has made so many of them! (It could, of course, just mean that people like procreating a lot…) Just as a mother of nine loves all of her children and doesn't want any to be estranged from the family, so God longs to be in relationship with all of us— to have a big party with us, in fact:

The kingdom of heaven may be compared to a king who gave a wedding banquet for his son. He sent his slaves to call those who had been invited to the wedding banquet, but they would not come… Then he said to his slaves, 'The wedding is ready, but those invited were not worthy. Go therefore into the main streets, and invite everyone you find to the wedding banquet.' Those slaves went out into the streets and gathered all whom they found, both good and bad; so the wedding hall was filled with guests. (Matthew 22:1–3, 8–10)

'Both good and bad'—that reminds me of the local scrap metal collector who has two sons. (This is a bit of a prodigal son story for today.) With one son the father has always been friends, but the other set up metal collecting in competition to his father, so the father fell out with him. We used to call them 'the good son and the bad son' (the good son's son worked with my husband for a while). Now the father has retired and the 'bad' son has taken over the business, and they appear to be reconciled. Ultimately, a good parent loves all his children, 'good' or 'bad'. God lets the rain fall on the just and the unjust:

But I say to you, Love your enemies and pray for those who persecute you, so that you may be children of your Father in heaven; for he makes his sun rise on the evil and on the good, and sends rain on the righteous and on the unrighteous. (Matthew 5:44–45)

I'll let you decide which one you are. Either way, God's love for you does not change.

Chapter 10

The next generation

An announcement

It was Christmas Eve 1993. Ed and I were at my parents' house, having our first Austrian-style festive meal. When the food was served and there was a moment to talk, I said to my parents, 'Well, do you think you are ready to be grandparents? (They were 78 and 80 at that point.) 'To whom?' asked my mother. 'To your grandchild.' And then we told them the news. It had been very hard keeping quiet until then, even on the day I went over to their house to help my dad decorate their tree, and he asked, 'Is that stomach upset you had getting better?', but I managed it. That was one of the happiest Christmases we have ever had.

In this Chapter I talk about a situation I have not actually experienced yet: when your children become parents themselves. Since my son is only 16, I haven't even experienced him having a life partner yet.

I haven't yet become a mother-in-law but I have seen my mother being one, and have had two mothers-in-law myself as, after Ed's mother died, his father remarried. Being 'the mother-in-law', as I've observed it in others, is not generally an easy situation for either side of the relationship (unless you're Asian, in which case you often rule the roost). What if my son marries someone with whom I don't get on? What if she sees me as an enemy? I can only hope that I get one of those rare situations in which mother-in-law and daughter-in-law live in perfect harmony. As my record on not being an interfering mother is not that good (John's just at the stage where he frequently exclaims, 'Stop mothering me!'), I'm not sure my record as a mother-in-law will be that much better.

Being a grandparent is a much more enticing prospect— grandparents are those lucky people who can enjoy a child, break all the parents' rules while the child is with them, and then hand it back! As a sign on a car said, 'If I had known how much easier grandchildren are, I'd have had them first.' I also have anxieties about the idea of my son's having children, as there is a high risk one or more of them might have an autism spectrum condition, perhaps more severe than my son has.

I'm getting ahead of myself here. Anyway, what does any of this have to do with our relationship with God? Well, I think there are some parallels.

Jesus commanded his followers to 'go and make disciples' (Matthew 28:19) all over the world. I'm not very good at this. I remember a colleague in a past job saying to me, 'You know that moment when you have just led someone to the Lord and you're wondering, "What can I give them to read to help them grow in faith"?' Er… no, I didn't. I had never, and still have never, knowingly led someone to the Lord. That's probably why that colleague is now a bishop and I'm not. This is not to say I haven't influenced people, and I have never made a secret of my faith. I'm just not an evangelist— I'm a writer.

Notice what Jesus didn't say: 'Go and make converts.' He said 'disciples', and disciples are people who are in a process of learning that never ends. I can hope that some things I've written have helped people in their discipleship, and from the letters I receive, I think that is not a vain hope.

There is a sense in which this is a similar process to having children: the baby arrives, but then there's a decade's long process of teaching it to live in relation to others: what we call 'discipline' in a family context, and 'discipling' in a church context. Then your grown child is ready to repeat the whole process with their own children, and so the population grows. Likewise, in your Christian life you hope that the disciples you make will then go on to make other disciples, and so the church—but more importantly, the kingdom of God—grows.

Some of us can't have our own children or grandchildren. Maybe that's similar to my complete failure to be an evangelist. Some may have no children physically, but many 'children in the Lord' as preachers, church mentors or Sunday school teachers. Paul regarded Timothy as his 'son in the Lord', although we do not know whether he had biological children of his own or even whether he was married: 'Paul, an apostle of Christ Jesus by the command of God our Saviour and of Christ Jesus our hope, To Timothy, my loyal child in the faith' (1 Timothy 1:1). Paul fulfilled his role as Timothy's 'father' in the faith, by sending him letters of support and guidance that still influence our churches today.

Some children will be birthed by one person and brought up by another. Also, there are those of us, like me, who are not gifted in calling people to be children of God but are able then to teach them what their new status means in terms of their lifestyle. This is perhaps like being an adoptive or a foster parent. I have long said that my little congregation is gifted at being a 'foster parent church': we take people who may have been wounded or dissatisfied by other churches, who may have almost given up on church, and we restore and heal them, and teach them our Anabaptist theology and ways—and then they move on and take those insights to other churches.

Like father, like son

They say that God has no grandchildren, and that is true in the sense that children of Christian parents have to come to faith for themselves and not just rely on their parents' faith. There is also a sense in which God does have grandchildren, and great-grandchildren, and great-great… well, you get the picture. One person (or a group of people) comes to Jesus, and then they in turn introduce other people to him, and so the generations go on. This is why we need to consider seriously what kind of spiritual heritage we are giving to the believers who come after us, whether they are our biological or spiritual children.

Because we are the people who brought our children up, when they have children they will, knowingly or unknowingly, reproduce in their own parenting many of the ways and words we used in our own parenting of them. This is one reason why it is so important to give them a good example. There are of course grown children who swear that with their own children they will do everything quite differently from the way their parents did—and sometimes this is a good thing. However, it is not so easy to break away. I have often caught myself sounding exactly like my own mother, even in ways in which I swore I would never copy my mother!

Very similar things happen with 'spiritual parenting'. The late great youth worker and writer Mike Yaconelli used to say, 'What you win them with is what you win them to.' (He is much missed, but fortunately he has a son, Mark Yaconelli, who, I think, looks exactly like him, sounds exactly like him, and says the same sort of liberating things his father used to say—which kind of proves my point.)

In other words, if you evangelise people by threats of hell

fire and an angry God, that is the sort of faith which with they are most likely to continue. Perhaps less extremely, if you bring them to faith by focusing exclusively on belief, if you effectively teach people that we are saved by what we believe, then that is probably the sort of religion they will have: one that is focussed almost entirely on getting your doctrine right, and in which discipleship consists mainly of avoiding a list of sins rather than becoming a Christ-like person. The Bible says we are saved by grace through faith, not that we have to believe six impossible things before breakfast like the Red Queen in *Alice Through the Looking Glass*,[1] in order to be saved. When Jesus healed people and said, 'Your faith has made you well' (see, for example, Matthew 9:22; Mark 10:52), he was not talking about their ability to understand penal substitution but their trust in Jesus as one sent by God.

This is what Hebrews says about the belief requirements for a relationship with God: 'Whoever would approach [God] must believe that he exists and that he rewards those who seek him' (11:6). These are not a very complex set of requirements! By contrast, we often set up a system of obligations that people must meet to be accepted as a 'real' Christian: they must be able to name the date on which they were converted; they must understand how Jesus died for our sins; they must believe in the Trinity; they must read a certain type of book and use a certain set of Bible reading notes...

We have to be careful that we are not like the Pharisees, to whom Jesus declared, 'Woe to you, scribes and Pharisees, hypocrites! For you cross sea and land to make a single convert, and you make the new convert twice as much a child of hell as yourselves' (Matthew 23:15). So often, in their early days as disciples, new Christians are taught all kinds of rules that they may then have to unlearn later. We should be teaching them how to follow Jesus, not how to be acceptable in our own denomination. I've had a lot of contact recently with people who have left the sect in which my husband grew up, a sect in which right doctrine is held as vitally important, and whose members speak of 'being in the truth'. These ex-members talk about their confusion when they left, and the way they had to learn a whole different way of being a Christian—and of course some didn't want anything more to do with faith of any kind. The sad thing is that some of them will end up in mainstream churches that are equally focused on correct doctrine as the sect was, just with a different set of doctrines. Even sadder, I personally think, is that the sect's doctrines are in my view more biblical than what passes for biblical doctrine in the majority of mainstream churches!

New ways

My parents-in-law are still part of this sect. One thing I do notice is that the younger generation—my husband's sister and brother-in-law and their grown-up daughters—are much more open to the idea that people who believe and live differently from them are just as Christian as they are.

The world changes with every new generation, and some-times the new generation rediscovers something that everyone knew, a few generations back. My mother used cloth nappies on me and my brother; I used nothing but disposables on my baby, and the next generation is going back to cloth again to protect the environment.

Likewise, the church is always changing from generation to generation, although sometimes the pace of change is decidedly slower than that of the society around it. 'Like a mighty tortoise moves the church of God; brothers, we are treading where our fathers trod,' goes a parody of a popular hymn.[2] (The original hymn starts with the words, 'Like a mighty army' and goes on to say, 'We are treading where the saints have trod.') There are always those who panic at the thought of change and think the new generation of believers are on a slippery slope to complete apostasy. The result is sometimes a church split, when one party carries on with the process of change, and the other digs its heels in and consolidates its hold on what it calls 'tradition'. I think you can tell from my language that I am generally in favour of the side that wants change—that is, until the proposed change is to some tradition that I hold particularly dear! We all have some matters in which we would like to see that (in the words of another hymn) 'nothing changes here'.[3]

But the world changes, and, to meet its needs and challenge it where it needs challenging, the church has to change too. Rather more rarely than I would wish, the church is sometimes actually ahead of society—for instance, the early church led the way on the unity of Jews and Gentiles, breaking down the ethnic and religious barriers that separated the two communities.

Every new generation in the church will want to do things differently—sometimes very differently, as in the 'emerging church' movement—and this will inevitably be a source of tension between older and younger generations. In much the same way, grandparents often frown on the way their children are bringing up their own children, and conflict can often erupt as a result. I am still trying to convince my mother that my son's Asperger's syndrome is not something he will grow out of with the right parenting!

Those of us who are older (and I'm rapidly entering that class!) have to accept that 'the way we did it in our time' may have its faults and lacks, that none of us parent, or do church, perfectly, because we are not perfect people, and that there will always be some things that are open to improvement, as well as some vital lessons that may get forgotten for a bit.

My mother, bringing up children in the 1950s, read a so-called 'child expert' called Dr Truby King, who insisted that you should never pick up a baby when it cries (which seems to me now a bit like child abuse). Those were the days when you left the pram out in the snow because fresh air was good for babies!

My generation, the baby boomers, rejected the way the previous generation parented, with lots of rules and commands and the expectation that children would obey their parents. My contemporaries mostly read Dr Spock and were convinced that any restriction at all we placed on our children would warp them for life. Children had to be free! We wanted to let our children grow up naturally, unhindered by parental restrictions. There were some good things in the approach— after all, children are not servants of their parents. But neither are parents servants of their children, and by the time I had my son at the age of 41, the pendulum had already swung back to recognising that children need boundaries. Now we were all reading Miriam Stoppard, who offered a balance between the two extremes that had preceded her (although for some reason she strongly disapproved of baby powder). The child-rearing experts of each time have a lot to answer for.

Maybe it's the same in the church. Maybe one generation will have a strong emphasis on our sinfulness and the holiness of God, and our need for the sacrifice of Jesus to appease God's wrath. Their hymns will be full of doctrine, their worship highly structured and ritualistic (even the 'low' churches have their own rituals), and their view of discipleship will focus heavily on rules and obedience. Then the next generation rebels against this, emphasising the fatherly/motherly love of God, the free gift of grace, and discipleship as a free response to that love and a way of spreading the love to others. Their worship will be relaxed, participatory and informal. Neither is necessarily wrong; they can each justify their approach from the Bible. What they need to do is not to promote their own particular emphasis until the whole church follows it but to learn to listen to each other and to find that of God in each other. The Quakers have a lot to teach us here, in their belief that the light of God shines in everyone—we only have to find it.

Family likeness

I wrote in Chapter 2 that, while Christians are 'children of God' in a particular way, there is also a sense in which all humans can be called 'children of God', because all of us, Christian or not, were made in the first place as the image of God: 'So God created humankind in his image, in the image of God he created them; male and female he created them (Genesis 1:27).

Whatever we believe that image to consist of, at the very least this tells us that, because we are made by God, there is a family likeness between God and us. What we call 'salvation' is simply God's reclaiming what was always God's, and reshaping it into what it was always meant to be. (It might also tell us, in the second half of the verse, that the full image of God can only be reflected by male and female together, but that's a whole other argument.)

Julian of Norwich asserts that 'in every soul which will be saved, there is a godly will which never assents to sin, and never will'.[4] In other words, the image of God in each human being has never been completely erased. I find this very encouraging: it tells me that following Jesus is something I am really capable of, in the power of the Holy Spirit. Admittedly, Julian of Norwich doesn't pronounce on the souls who are not to be saved, but I believe that is only for God to do, not for us. We don't have the luxury—at least not this side of the judgment day—of deciding for ourselves who is in God's favour and who isn't:

He put before them another parable: 'The kingdom of heaven may be compared to someone who sowed good seed in his field; but while everybody was asleep, an enemy came and sowed weeds among the wheat, and then went away. So when the plants came up and bore grain, then the weeds appeared as well. And the slaves of the householder came and said to him, "Master, did you not sow good seed in your field? Where, then, did these weeds come from?" He answered, "An enemy has done this." The slaves said to him, "Then do you want us to go and gather them?" But he replied, "No; for in gathering the weeds you would uproot the wheat along with them. Let both of them grow together until the harvest; and at harvest time I will tell the reapers, Collect the weeds first and bind them in bundles to be burned, but gather the wheat into my barn."' (Matthew 13:24–30)

Jesus was talking of a particular type of weed that looked very like the crop until it was fully grown. We can often identify which of people's actions are good or evil, but we cannot reliably identify, until the judgment day, which people are among 'those who are to be saved' and which not. The best we can do, as the Quakers suggest, is to look for and encourage the best in any person, which is put there by God in making that person in God's image. John Swanson, writing on Julian of Norwich, says that Julian's main concern is not our redemption but our 'demption'.[5] I think what he means by this is that we belong just as much to God in our creation as we do in our redemption.

What does this mean for our consideration of God's parenthood and its resemblances to our parenthood? Well, we may be born as 'the image' of one or the other parent, but as we grow, we also become more like our parents in many other ways—hardly surprising since, all being well, we are brought up by them. For those brought up by adoptive parents, the story is more complicated: as well as looking genetically like their birth parents and in some ways acting like them, the child will also acquire some likeness to their adoptive parents. For instance, a child adopted by Christian parents is more likely to become a Christian than they might have if they grew up in their birth family.

If we are both 'birthed' by God in our creation, and 'born from above' in our redemption, we have a double chance of developing a family likeness to our divine parent. We have God-like capacities because of being made in God's image; and the process of salvation 'recaptures' those capacities corrupted by sin, makes them new, and increases our ability to use them well. This means that, if we are faithfully following Jesus:

All of us, with unveiled faces, seeing the glory of the Lord as though reflected in a mirror, are being transformed into the same image from one degree of glory to another; for this comes from the Lord, the Spirit. (2 Corinthians 3:18)

Because of this process, we are not only called God's children, we begin to look like God's children. The process goes on with the next generation—indeed grandchildren can be more like their grandparents than they are like their parents. Sometimes talents or character traits 'skip a generation'.

The most important thing to notice about this is that the process of becoming Christ-like is not a matter of a huge effort on our part to make ourselves like Jesus. We don't have to make ourselves become like our parents or grandparents—it just happens naturally. This is not just because of the genes we inherit from them, but because of the time we have spent with them from our very earliest, most impressionable years. Have you noticed how dogs seem to look like their owners (or is it the other way around)? Or happily married couples, from long togetherness, start to mimic each other's expressions and use each other's language? This is not a conscious, deliberate process. I didn't choose to look physically exactly like my father, but from my birth, nobody ever doubted who my father was—they only had to look at me! Nor have I chosen occasionally to be just like my mother. In fact, often I find I am acting or speaking just like her when I don't want to! It's simply inevitable, considering that I was both given birth by her and brought up by her.

As we spend time seeking God's presence and God's way for us, studying the 'history of God' that the Bible gives us, and making strong relationships with those who can teach us more of God, we inevitably become more like how God wants us to be. Then, in turn, we hope that others can see God in us, turn to God and learn from us what it means to be God's child and disciple—which brings us back to where this chapter started, with the birth of a new generation of people made in God's image and called to be God's imitators.

Conclusion

Good gifts

Here, as I explored in the last chapter, the internal image we have of God is key. Actually, most of this book is really an attempt to convince people, including myself, that God is not a stern, punitive Victorian father, but a parent who always wills the best for their children.

Although I have been thinking about this theme for some years, I have only recently connected it with this saying of Jesus:

'Is there anyone among you who, if your child asks for bread, will give a stone? Or if the child asks for a fish, will give a snake? If you then, who are evil, know how to give good gifts to your children, how much more will your Father in heaven give good things to those who ask him!' (Matthew 7:9–11)

When these verses came into my mind, I quickly realised that this book is essentially an extended meditation on this teaching of Jesus. Luke's version has God giving the Holy Spirit, rather than 'good things', which perhaps is a welcome corrective to our tendency to view God as a divine slot-machine, giving us whatever we want. In fact, these two versions are not contradictory, for all good things in our life come from the God, who is Spirit, and having the Holy Spirit within you certainly makes good things happen in your life: 'Every generous act of giving, with every perfect gift, is from above, coming down from the Father of lights, with whom there is no variation or shadow due to change' (James 1:17).

Viewing God as the unstinting giver, rather than as the demanding employer, affects the way we treat other people who are made in God's image. A person with a very disturbed home background, with neglectful or abusive parents, will find it hard to be generous and loving to others, and faithful in relationships, even if they want to be. Similarly, our image and experience of God moulds the way we worship, pray and live, negatively or positively. That is why it is so important to examine our own understanding of the character and the parenthood of God. If our view of God is that of a demanding dictator who rules us absolutely and will brook no questions, then that is the way we will treat those in our care, whether natural children or our congregation, if we are church leaders. If we think of God as an infinitely loving parent who wants God's children to be transformed into the very best God has made them to be, then we will encourage our children or our congregation to have a free, trusting relationship with God and to explore the gifts that God wants to give them.

If we are good parents, there are certain things we would never in a million years think of doing to our children: for instance, choosing one or two as our favourites and condemning the others from the moment they are born. Yet we attribute such actions to God, who is supposed to be the model for all parenthood. Are we not guilty of portraying God as 'a harsh man, reaping where [he] did not sow, and gathering where [he] did not scatter seed' (Matthew 25:24)?

All this reminds me of a Peanuts[1] cartoon in which it is raining heavily and Charlie Brown asks Linus whether there will be a universal flood. Linus replies that God promised Noah there would never again be a flood covering the earth (we read that passage in the last chapter). 'Thank you,' says Charlie Brown, 'you have taken a great weight off my mind.' 'Sound theology has a way of doing that,' replies Linus. I think it is sound theology to dwell more on God's sacrificial love than on God's uncompromising judgment—and it certainly takes a great load off my mind.

I have written this book to explore a more loving idea of God who, the letters of John tell us, is not only loving, but actually is love itself. This is the God I have found in my experience of being a parent, especially in being a parent of a child with a special need. I hope that you, whether you are a parent or not, whether you want to be or not, have found glimpses of that God within the pages of this book. I believe the message it attempts to convey is one that is vital for the life and growth of the church—and the world, which is God's—today.

Study questions
for groups and individuals

Chapter 1: Conception

Choose a partner, and share with each other your experience of, and feelings about, having or not having children, and where you find God in your situation. Rejoin the group, and share anything you want to from your discussion. (Those who don't wish to share should not be asked to do so.)

'"Father"… is God's name from eternity.' Do you agree with this statement? What emotions does it arouse in you?

Does the church adequately support those who are struggling with childlessness? Or does it put too much emphasis on families?

Chapter 2: Pregnancy and birth

What thoughts and feelings does the idea of God as mother arouse in you? Do you think seeing God as a mother is unbiblical, or a much-needed recovery of a forgotten perspective?

The chapter talks about a baby learning to recognise the smell of its mother, and perhaps the new Christian learning to recognise 'the smell of God'. Do you think this is a helpful metaphor? How do you think we do this?

'God is in the process of reproducing himself.' Do you think this is true? What difference might thinking this make to our faith?

Chapter 3: Growth and learning

'As our children grow, we take pleasure in their growing independence.' Do you think God also takes pleasure in our growth to maturity as a Christian? What does it mean to 'grow up into the full stature of Christ'?

'God's chief desire is not for what we do on a Sunday morning but for us to do God's will and serve God's kingdom from Monday to Saturday.' Do you agree? If so, how can we make church more relevant to our Monday-to-Saturday lives?

Do you believe God has ordained specific roles for men and women? Is this issue too divisive, or one that the church should address?

Chapter 4: Tears, tumbles and tantrums

'God is… a materialist.' What do you think is meant by this statement? Do you agree?

How do you explain sin and suffering in the world, to yourself or others? Is it even explainable? Does the experience of parenting shed any light on it?

Is every human being in some sense a child of God? Or is this status limited to Christians? What difference would seeing everyone as a child of God make to your faith?

Chapter 5: Something wrong

'We are all God's "special" children.' Do you agree with this? How is this different from saying 'we are all sinners', and which description do you prefer?

Do you think the current educational system works for children with special needs? What changes would you like to see? How, if at all, does this relate to your faith?

Which image resonates most for you: the idea that we are 'born… of God' (John 1:13) or the idea that we are 'adopted' by God (Galatians 4:5). Why do you prefer the one you do? Which do you think is most useful for evangelism?

Chapter 6: Discipline

Does God 'discipline' us? Is it helpful or unhelpful to see suffering as a discipline from God? What parallels can you see between how we discipline our children and how God disciplines us?

'Does God grieve at God's children being so little able to get on with each other?' What do you think? How might Christians of different traditions get on better?

'Could global justice… be a higher priority for God than whether we have our doctrines right or have the "right" views on personal morality?' Do you think the church sometimes focuses too much on personal ethics and not enough on global ethics?

Chapter 7: Teenage traumas

Do teenagers need to go through a period of rebellion? Does every Christian need to go through a period of questioning their faith?

Do you have problems talking to your children (if you have any) about sex? What do you think God's attitude is to sex?

What do you think it means to have a mature faith? How can churches promote maturity of faith?

Chapter 8: Making plans

What does God's guidance mean to you? Do you think God has every detail of our lives planned?

Do you believe in hell as eternal torture, or as destruction of evil, or do you not believe in hell at all? What difference does this make to your faith and life?

Would you like to be able to surprise God?

Chapter 9: The pain of love

Which character do you most identify with in the story of the prodigal son? Why?

Have you had, or do you have, a 'prodigal' in your own family? How have you coped with this?

What is your own, 'deep-down', image of God? Do you think it is accurate? Does this relate at all to how you see the cross of Jesus?

Chapter 10: The next generation

What are the most important values your parents, or people who acted as parents to you, pass on to you? What do you want your children (if you have any) to keep from you and pass on to their children?

Does the way you were brought up influence how you view God as a parent?

Name one thought you will take away with you from this book, and explain why.

Notes

Chapter 1: Conception

1   Kenneth McAll, *Healing the Family Tree*, Sheldon Press, 1999
2   Lewis Carroll, *Alice in Wonderland*, 1865, various editions
3   William Paul Young, *The Shack*, Hodder Faith, 2008

Chapter 2: Pregnancy and birth

1   Julian of Norwich, *Showings*, translated by Edmund Colledge and James Walsh, SPCK, 1978, p. 297

Chapter 3: Growth and learning

1   Kate Clanchy, 'Plain Work', in *Newborn*, Picador 2004

Chapter 4: Tears, tumbles and tantrums

1   Julian of Norwich, *Showings*, p. 301
2   Julian of Norwich, *Showings*, pp. 267–278
3   Alfred, Lord Tennyson, 'In Memoriam', from *Poems and Plays*, Oxford University Press, 1965
4   M. Scott Peck, Arrow Books, 1990, pp. 72–75
5   Irenaus, *Adversus Haereses (Against Heresies)*

Chapter 6: Discipline

1   Randolph K. Sanders, *A Parent's Bedside Companion: Inspiration for parents of young children* (Herald Press, 1994)
2   Julian of Norwich, *Showings*, p. 299

Chapter 7: Teenage traumas

1   James Fowler, *Stages of Faith: The Psychology of Human Development and the Quest for Meaning*, HarperCollins, 1995
2   M. Scott Peck, *The Different Drum: Community making and peace*, Simon & Schuster, 1987, and *Further Along the Road Less Travelled*, Simon and Schuster, 1993

3 Julian of Norwich, *Showings*, p. 264

4 Walter Wangerin, *Father and Son*, Zondervan, 2008

Chapter 8: Making plans

1 I recommend *What Does the Bible Really Say about Hell?* by Randy Klassen (Pandora Press, 2001).

2 David Runcorn, *Choice, Desire and the Will of God: What more do you want?*, SPCK, 2003, pp. 9–10

Chapter 9: The pain of love

1 Antoine de Saint-Exupéry, *The Little Prince*, translated by Katherine Woods, Harcourt, 1943, 1971

2 Gerard Hughes, *God of Surprises*, Darton, Longman and Todd, 1985

Chapter 10: The next generation

1 Lewis Carroll, *Alice Through the Looking Glass*, 1871, various editions

2 Sabine Baring-Gould, 'Onward Christian soldiers', 1865

3 Anna Laetitia Waring, 'In heavenly love abiding', 1850

4 Julian of Norwich, *Showings*, p. 241

5 John Swanson OJN, in Robert Llewellyn (ed.), *Julian: Woman of Our Day* (DLT, 1985)

Conclusion

1 Robert L. Short, *The Gospel According to Peanuts*, Westminster John Knox Press, 1965

Enjoyed

this book?

Write a review—we'd love to hear what you think.
Email: reviews@brf.org.uk

Keep up to date—receive details of our new books as they happen.
Sign up for email news and select your interest groups at:
www.brfonline.org.uk/findoutmore/

Follow us on Twitter @brfonline

By post—to receive new title information by post (UK only), complete
the form below and post to: BRF Mailing Lists, 15 The Chambers, Vineyard,
Abingdon, Oxfordshire, OX14 3FE

Your Details
Name _____
Address_____
_____
Town/City _____ Post Code _____
Email_____

Your Interest Groups (*Please tick as appropriate)	
☐ Advent/Lent	☐ Messy Church
☐ Bible Reading & Study	☐ Pastoral
☐ Children's Books	☐ Prayer & Spirituality
☐ Discipleship	☐ Resources for Children's Church
☐ Leadership	☐ Resources for Schools

Support your local bookshop
Ask about their new title information schemes.